CHILDREN'S ENCYCLOPEDIA
ANIMALS

CHILDREN'S ENCYCLOPEDIA
ANIMALS

Miles Kelly

First published in 2014 by Miles Kelly Publishing Ltd
Harding's Barn, Bardfield End Green, Thaxted, Essex, CM6 3PX, UK

Copyright © Miles Kelly Publishing Ltd 2014

2 4 6 8 10 9 7 5 3 1

Publishing Director Belinda Gallagher
Creative Director Jo Cowan
Cover Designer Simon Lee
Designers Angela Ashton, D&A, Rob Hale, Sally Lace,
Andrea Slane, Elaine Wilkinson
Editors Fran Bromage, Amy Johnson,
Sarah Parkin, Claire Philip
Indexer Jane Parker
Image Manager Liberty Newton
Production Manager Elizabeth Collins
Reprographics Stephan Davis, Jennifer Cozens, Thom Allaway
Contributors Camilla de la Bedoyere, Jinny Johnson,
Ann Kay, Steve Parker

ISBN 978-1-78209-498-2

Printed in China

British Library Cataloguing-in-Publication Data
A catalogue record for this book is available from the British Library

Made with paper from a sustainable forest

www.mileskelly.net
info@mileskelly.net

CONTENTS

BUGS

8-49

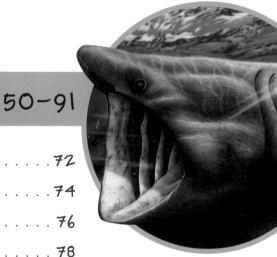

SHARKS

50-91

REPTILES AND AMPHIBIANS 92–133

BIRDS

MAMMALS

BUGS

1 Insects are among the most numerous and widespread animals on Earth. They form the largest of all animal groups, with millions of different kinds, or species, which live almost everywhere in the world. But not all creepy-crawlies are insects. Spiders belong to a different group called arachnids, and millipedes are in yet another group.

► Cockchafers are insects, as shown by their wings and six legs. Also called chafers, cockchafers belong to the largest subgroup of insects, the beetles.

Insects everywhere

2 **The housefly is one of the most common, widespread and annoying insects.** There are many other members of the fly group, such as bluebottles, horseflies, craneflies and fruitflies. They all have two wings. Most other kinds of insects have four wings.

▼ Insects, such as this horsefly, do not have a bony skeleton like we do. Their bodies are covered by horny plates, called an exoskeleton.

Wings are clear or with a yellowish tinge

Dark colouring

Large, stocky body, 1–2.5 centimetres long

Short antennae

Very large eyes, which are widely separated in females, but joined in males

3 **The ladybird is a noticeable insect with its bright red or yellow body, and black spots.** It is a member of the beetle group – the biggest insect group of all. There are more than half a million kinds, from massive Goliath beetles to tiny flea beetles.

▶ Bright colours warn other animals that ladybirds taste horrible.

5 **The cabbage white butterfly is not usually welcome in the garden.** Its young, known as caterpillars, eat the leaves of plants. There are thousands of kinds of butterflies, and even more kinds of their night-time cousins, the moths.

▼ When the earwig is threatened, it raises its tail to try to make itself look bigger.

4 **The earwig is a familiar insect outside – and sometimes inside.** Despite their name, earwigs do not crawl into ears or hide in wigs, but they do like dark, damp corners. Earwigs form one of the smaller insect groups, with fewer than 2000 different kinds.

6 Ants are fine in the garden or wood, but are pests in the house. Ants, bees and wasps make up a large insect group with some 130,000 different kinds. Most can sting, although many are too small to hurt people. However, some types, such as bulldog ants, have a painful bite.

▶ Ants use their antennae and sense of touch as a means of communication. These ants are forming a 'living bridge' so their fellow workers can cross a gap to reach food.

7 The scorpionfly has a nasty-looking sting on a long curved tail. It flies or crawls around bushes and weeds during summer. Only the male scorpionfly has the red tail. It looks like the sting of a scorpion, but is harmless.

SPOT THE INSECTS!
Have you seen any insects so far today? Maybe a fly whizzing around the house or a butterfly flitting among the flowers? On a warm summer's day you will probably spot lots of different insects. On a cold winter's day there are fewer insects about – most are hiding away or have not hatched out of their eggs.

How insects grow

8 Nearly all insects begin life inside an egg. The female insect usually lays her eggs in an out-of-the-way place, such as under a stone, leaf or bark, or in the soil.

▼ The scarlet lily beetle lays her eggs directly onto the lily leaves, which the grubs will eat when they hatch.

I DON'T BELIEVE IT!

Courtship is a dangerous time for the male praying mantis. The female is much bigger than the male and, as soon as they have mated, she may eat him!

9 Usually a female insect mates with a male insect before she can lay her eggs. The female and male come together to check they are both the same kind of insect and are healthy. This is known as courtship. Butterflies often flit through the air together in a 'courtship dance'.

10 When some types of insects hatch, they do not look like their parents. A young beetle, butterfly or fly is soft-bodied, wriggly and worm-like. This young stage is called a larva. A beetle larva is called a grub, a butterfly larva is a caterpillar and a fly larva is a maggot.

◄ Large caterpillars always eat into the centre of the leaf from the edge. Caterpillars grasp the leaf with their legs, while their specially developed front jaws chew their food.

① The butterfly swallows air, expands its body and splits its chrysalis open

② It struggles free of the casing

③ The butterfly clings to the chrysalis

④ Blood is pumped into the wings, which stretch and stiffen

⑤ In half an hour, the wings are full size. Once dry, the butterfly is able to fly

▲ This viceroy butterfly is emerging from its chrysalis.

11 The larva eats and eats. It sheds its skin several times so it can grow. Then it changes into the next stage of its life, called a pupa. The pupa has a hard outer case that stays still and inactive. Inside, the larva is changing shape again – this is known as metamorphosis.

12 At last the pupa's case splits open and the adult insect crawls out. Its body, legs and wings spread out and harden. Now the insect is ready to find food and a mate.

13 Some kinds of insects change shape less as they grow. When a cricket or grasshopper hatches, it looks similar to its parents, but it may not have wings.

14 The young cricket eats and eats, and sheds (or moults) its skin several times as it grows. Each time it looks more like its parent. A young insect that resembles an adult is called a nymph. At the last moult it becomes a fully formed adult, ready to feed and breed.

◄ Most crickets, as well as grasshoppers and locusts, moult between five and eight times before adulthood.

Getting about

15 An insect's wings are attached to the middle part of its body, the thorax. This is like a box with strong walls, called a clickbox. Muscles pull to make the walls click in and out, which in turn makes the wings flick up and down. A large butterfly flaps its wings once or twice each second. Some tiny flies flap almost 1000 times each second.

16 Most kinds of insects have two pairs of wings and use them to fly from place to place. One of the strongest fliers is the Apollo butterfly of Europe and Asia. It flies high over hills and mountains, then rests on a rock or flower in the sunshine.

17 The smallest fliers include gnats, midges and mosquitoes. These are true flies, with one pair of wings. Some are almost too tiny for us to see. Certain types bite animals and people, sucking their blood as food.

◄ Apollo butterflies flit between plants, searching for sweet nectar to drink.

18 A few insects lack wings. They are mostly very small and live in the soil, such as bristletails and certain aphids. One kind of bristletail is the silverfish – a small, shiny, fast-running insect.

▲ Dragonflies catch prey in a 'basket' formed by their legs.

19 A fast and fierce flying hunter is the dragonfly. Its huge eyes spot tiny prey such as midges and mayflies. The dragonfly dashes through the air, turns at speed, grabs the victim and flies back to a perch to eat its meal.

► Silverfish are nocturnal, which means they are mainly active at night.

20 Some insects flash bright lights as they fly. The firefly is not a fly, but a type of beetle. Male fireflies 'dance' in the air at dusk, the rear parts of their bodies glowing on and off about once each second. Female fireflies stay on twigs and leaves, and glow in reply as part of their courtship.

▼ Each kind of firefly has its own pattern of flashes.

QUIZ

1. How many wings do most insects have?
2. Where on its body are an insect's wings attached?
3. Which part of the firefly glows in the dark?

Answers:
1. Two pairs
2. Its middle, called the thorax
3. Rear parts

Champion leapers

21 Many insects move around mainly by hopping and jumping, rather than flying. They have long, strong legs and can leap great distances, especially to avoid enemies and escape from danger. Grasshoppers are up to 15 centimetres long and some types can jump more than 3 metres. The grasshopper often opens its brightly patterned wings briefly as it leaps, giving a flash of colour.

22 The springtail jumps with its tail, rather than its legs. The rear part of its body is shaped like a V or Y. It is folded under the body until it flicks down and flips the insect through the air. Springtails are as long as this letter 'l' but some can leap more than 5 centimetres!

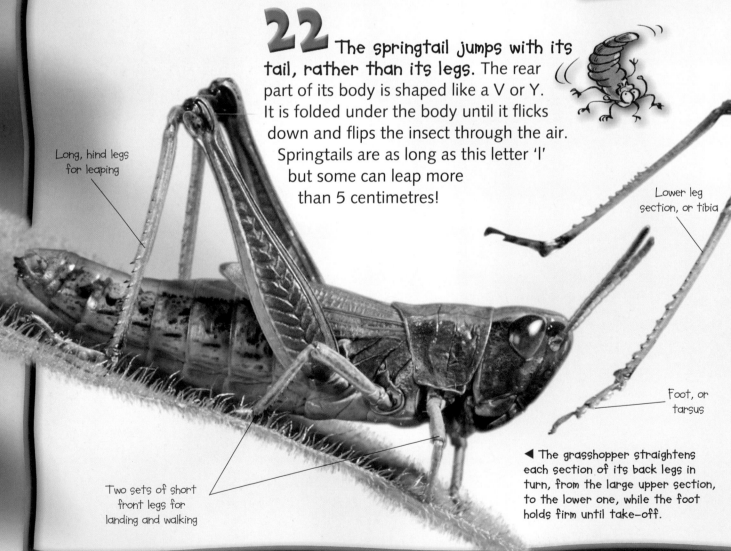

Long, hind legs for leaping

Two sets of short front legs for landing and walking

Lower leg section, or tibia

Foot, or tarsus

◄ The grasshopper straightens each section of its back legs in turn, from the large upper section, to the lower one, while the foot holds firm until take-off.

▲ Froghoppers take just one five-hundredth of a second to get airborne.

23 The greatest insect jumpers for their size are fleas, and also the froghopper. This small sap-sucking bug can leap over 70 centimetres high – more than 100 times its own body length.

Large eyes to focus on where to land

Wings folded against body

Upper leg section, or femur

QUIZ

1. Does the springtail jump using its head or tail?
2. How high is a froghopper able to leap?
3. What does a click beetle do when it's in danger?

Answers:
1. Uses its tail 2. 100 times its own body length 3. It plays dead

② Arches its body and flicks up

③ Lands right way up on leaf

① Click beetle plays dead

24 The click beetle, or skipjack, is another insect leaper. This beetle is about 12 millimetres long. When it is in danger it falls on its back and pretends to be dead. When the danger has passed, it slowly arches its body and straightens with a 'click'. It can flick itself about 25 centimetres into the air!

◀ The 'click' is from a joint between the first and second thorax parts.

▶ Cockroaches are expert scavengers, able to live on tiny scraps of our food. Some kinds spread germs in their droppings.

25 Some insects rarely fly or leap. They prefer to run and run... all day, and sometimes all night too. Among the champion insect runners are cockroaches. There are about 4500 different kinds and they are tough and adaptable. Some live in soil or caves, but most scurry speedily across the ground and dart into narrow crevices, under logs, stones, cupboards – even beds!

26 One of the busiest insect walkers is the devil's coach-horse, which resembles an earwig. It belongs to the group known as rove beetles, which walk huge distances to find food.

▼ The devil's coach-horse has powerful mouthparts to tear apart small caterpillars, grubs and worms.

27 Some insects can run along smooth slippery surfaces, such as walls, windows or wet rocks. Others can run along the beds of ponds and rivers. The stonefly nymph has big, strong, wide-splayed legs that grip even smooth stones in rushing streams.

◄ The stonefly nymph, the larva of the stonefly, scuttles over wet rocks and riverbeds searching for food.

28 The green tiger beetle is an active hunter. It races over open ground, chasing smaller creatures such as ants, woodlice, worms and little spiders. It has huge jaws for its size and rips apart any victim.

I DON'T BELIEVE IT!

Green tiger beetles are about 12–15 millimetres long but can run at about 60–70 centimetres per second. That is like a human sprinter running 100 metres in one second!

Watery wonders

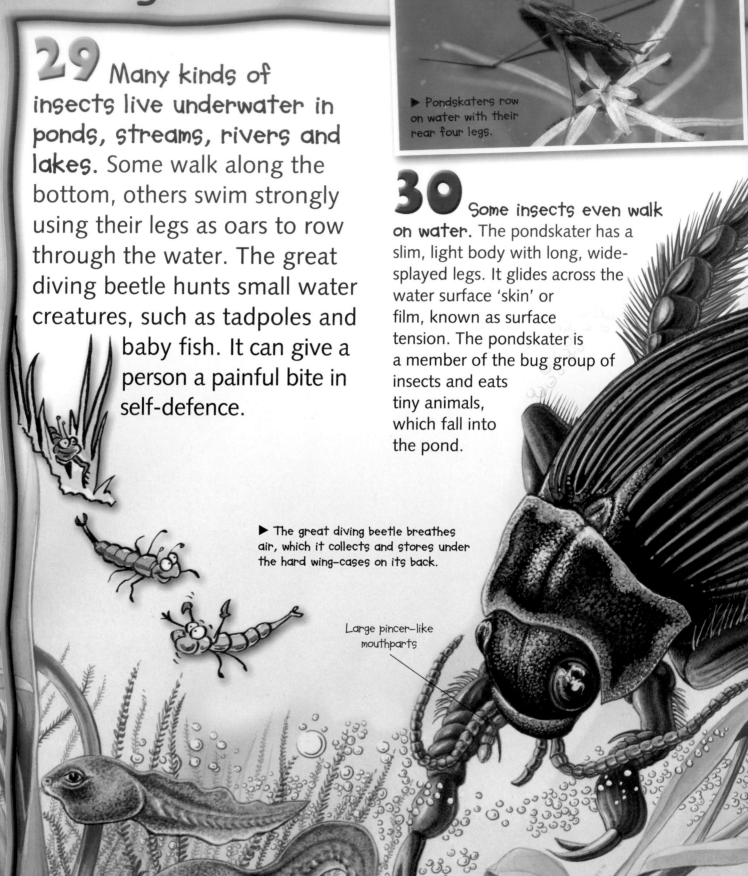

29 Many kinds of insects live underwater in ponds, streams, rivers and lakes. Some walk along the bottom, others swim strongly using their legs as oars to row through the water. The great diving beetle hunts small water creatures, such as tadpoles and baby fish. It can give a person a painful bite in self-defence.

► Pondskaters row on water with their rear four legs.

30 Some insects even walk on water. The pondskater has a slim, light body with long, wide-splayed legs. It glides across the water surface 'skin' or film, known as surface tension. The pondskater is a member of the bug group of insects and eats tiny animals, which fall into the pond.

► The great diving beetle breathes air, which it collects and stores under the hard wing-cases on its back.

Large pincer-like mouthparts

INVESTIGATE

With help from a grown-up, fill a bowl of water and let the water settle. Investigate what you can place on top of the water that doesn't break the water tension. Try laying paper, plastic or grass on the water. What happens?

Partly formed wings

◄ A damselfly nymph hunts tiny water creatures, including other insect nymphs.

Smooth, hard wing-cases keeps the beetle streamlined

Feathery gills

Hairs on legs help the diving beetle to swim

31 The nymphs of dragonflies, damselflies, stoneflies and mayflies have tails with feathery gills. These work like the gills of a fish, and help the nymph breath underwater. These young insects do not need to go to the surface until they change into adults.

32 Some water insects, such as the great silver water beetle, breathe air. They must come to the surface for fresh air supplies. The hairs on the beetle's body then trap tiny bubbles of air for breathing below.

Brilliant burrowers

33 Soil teems with millions of creatures – and many are insects. Some are larvae or grubs, others are fully-grown insects, such as burrowing beetles, ants, termites and earwigs. These soil insects are a vital source of food for all kinds of larger animals, from spiders and shrews to moles and birds.

34 The larva of the click beetle is shiny orange, up to 25 millimetres long and called a **wireworm**. It stays undergound, feeding on plant parts, for up to five years. Then it changes into an adult and leaves the soil. Wireworms can be serious pests of crops such as barley, oats, wheat, potatoes and beet.

▶ Many insects pose a threat to farmers' crops. Farmers can use pesticides – chemicals to kill the insects – but many people think that this harms other plants and animals.

35

The larva of the cranefly ('daddy long-legs') is called a leatherjacket because of its tough, leathery skin. Leatherjackets eat the roots of grasses, including cereal crops, such as wheat. They hatch from their eggs in late summer and feed in the soil. They change into pupae and then adults the following summer.

INSECT LARVAE

1 African fruit beetle larva
2 Black cutworm caterpillar
3 Cicada grub
4 Click beetle larva
5 Cockchafer grub
6 Leatherjacket
7 Japanese beetle larva

ADULT INSECTS

1 African fruit beetle
2 Black cutworm moth
3 Cicada
4 Click beetle
5 Cockchafer
6 Cranefly
7 Japanese beetle

36

The larva of the cicada may live underground for more than ten years. Different types of cicadas stay in the soil for different periods of time. The American periodic cicada is probably the record holder, taking 17 years to change into a pupa and then an adult. Adults make loud chirping or buzzing sounds.

▶ Adult cicadas suck the sap of bushes and trees.

Bloodthirsty bugs

37 Although most insects are small, they are among the fiercest hunters in the animal world. Many have huge mouthparts shaped like spears or saws, for grabbing and tearing up victims. Some actively chase after prey, while others lie in wait and surprise it.

Powerful jaws for digging and cutting up food

▲ Insect jaws, or mandibles, like this wasp's, move from side-to-side.

38 The antlion larva digs small pits in sand or loose soil. It hides below the surface at the bottom of the pit and waits for small creatures to wander past and slip in. The larva then grasps them with its fang-like mouthparts.

39 The lacewing looks delicate and dainty, but it is a fearsome hunter. It hunts aphids such as greenfly and blackfly, and drinks their body fluids. It may also have a sip of sweet, sugary nectar from a flower.

▼ The lacewing is green to blend in with the leaves where it hunts.

40 One of the most powerful insect predators is the praying mantis. It gets its name from the way it holds its front legs folded, like a person with hands together in prayer. The front legs have sharp spines, and snap together like spiky scissors to grab prey, such as moths or caterpillars.

◄ The mantis stays perfectly still, camouflaged by its body colouring, which blends in with the leaf or flower where it waits. When a victim comes near – SNAP!

QUIZ

1. What does a wasp use its jaws for?

2. Finish the name of this insect: praying...?

3. Which insect's larva digs small pits in sand?

Answers:
1. Digging and cutting up food 2. Mantis 3. Antlion

25

Veggie bugs

◄ Mealybugs, scale insects and aphids can be serious pests in vegetable fields, orchards and greenhouses.

▲ Most shield bugs feed on plant sap using their sucking mouth parts.

41 About nine out of ten kinds of insects eat some kind of plant food. Many feed on soft, rich, nutritious substances. These include the sap in stems and leaves, the mineral-rich liquid in roots, the nectar in flowers and the soft flesh of squashy fruits and berries.

42 Solid wood may not seem very tasty, but many kinds of insects eat it. They usually consume the wood when they are larvae or grubs, making tunnels as they eat their way through trees, logs and timber structures, such as bridges, fences, houses and furniture.

► Woodworms are various kinds of wood-eating beetle larvae. Some stay in the wood for three years or more.

43 Animal droppings are delicious to many kinds of insects. Various types of beetles lay their eggs in warm, steamy piles of droppings. When the larvae hatch out, they eat the dung.

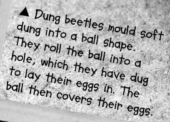

▲ Dung beetles mould soft dung into a ball shape. They roll the ball into a hole, which they have dug to lay their eggs in. The ball then covers their eggs.

◄ A lacebug jabs its sharp mouthparts into a plant to suck up the rich, syrupy sap inside.

44 Insects are not fussy eaters! They feed on old bits of damp and crumbling wood, dying trees, brown and decaying leaves and smelly, rotting fruit. This is nature's way of recycling goodness and nutrients in old plant parts, and returning them to the soil so new trees and other plants can grow.

▲ Fruitworms are insect larvae that may be moth caterpillars or beetle grubs, as shown here.

Stings and things

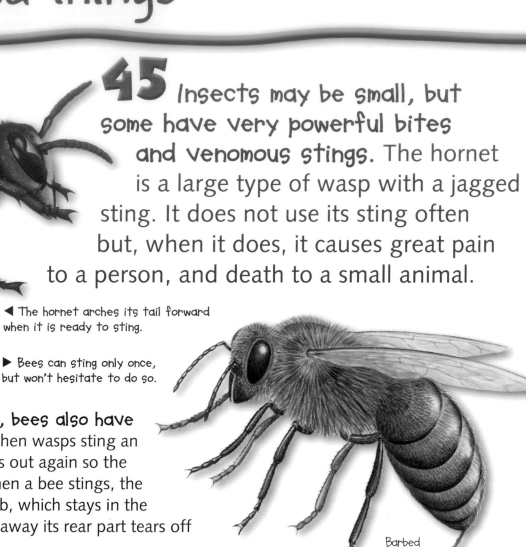

45 Insects may be small, but some have very powerful bites and venomous stings. The hornet is a large type of wasp with a jagged sting. It does not use its sting often but, when it does, it causes great pain to a person, and death to a small animal.

◄ The hornet arches its tail forward when it is ready to sting.

► Bees can sting only once, but won't hesitate to do so.

Jagged sting on rear end

46 Like wasps, bees also have a venomous sting. When wasps sting an enemy, the sting comes out again so the wasp can fly away. When a bee stings, the sting has a hook or barb, which stays in the victim. As the bee flies away its rear part tears off and the bee soon dies.

Barbed stinger

Downward-pointing fangs

47 The tarantula spiders called bird-eaters really do eat birds. They inject their venom into their prey with large fangs. As well as birds, they eat mice, frogs and even small snakes.

◄ The king baboon spider is a big tarantula from Africa, which measures 20 centimetres across from leg to leg.

48 To startle and sting an attacker, the bombardier beetle squirts out a spray of hot liquid. It comes out of its rear end like a spray gun and gives the beetle time to escape.

▼ Army ants march and feed by day, then gather in a clump-like 'living nest' or bivouac to rest at night.

49 One army ant can give a small bite, but 10,000 ants are much more dangerous. Army ants are mainly from South America and do not stay in a nest like other ants. They march in long lines through the forest, eating whatever they can bite, sting and overpower, from large spiders to lizards and birds.

Clever colonies

50 Some insects live together in huge groups called colonies, which are like insect cities. There are four main types of insects that form colonies. One is the termites. The other three are all in the same insect subgroup and are bees, wasps and ants.

▶ An ants' nest is packed with tunnels and chambers.

51 Different kinds of ants make nests from whatever material is available. Ants might use mud, small sticks and twigs, tiny bits of stone and gravel, or chewed-up pieces of leaves and flowers.

Winged males and females leave to start their own nests

52 Leafcutter ants grow their own food. They harvest leaves to use in the nest to grow fungi, which they eat.

53 In most insect colonies, only one or two members lay eggs. These are the queens and they are usually much bigger than the other ants. A queen can lay over 100 eggs each day.

The queen lays eggs in a separate chamber

Nursery chamber with ant larvae

▼ This wasp is making new cells for larvae.

54 A wasps' nest will have about 5000 wasps in it, but these are small builders in the insect world! A termite colony may have more than 5,000,000 inhabitants! Wood ants form nests of up to 300,000. Honeybees number around 50,000, while bumblebees live in colonies of only 10 or 20.

I DON'T BELIEVE IT!

Ants look after aphids and milk them like cows! They stroke the aphids to obtain a sugary liquid called honeydew, which the ants sip to get energy.

Worker ants care for the eggs and larvae

55 Inside an ants' nest are many kinds of workers, each with different jobs to do. Foragers tunnel into the soil and collect food, such as bits of plants and animals. Guards at the entrances to the nest bite any animals that try to come in. Nursery workers look after the eggs, larvae and pupae, while courtiers feed and clean the queen.

Where am I?

56 Insects have some of the best types of camouflage in the world. Camouflage is when a living thing blends in with its surroundings, so it is difficult to notice. This makes it hard for predators to see it. Or, if the insect is a predator, camouflage helps it to stalk its prey unnoticed.

57 The thornbug has a hard, pointed body casing. It sits still on a twig pretending to be a real thorn. It moves about and feeds at night.

▲ Thornbugs stay completely still during the daytime.

The 'thorn' is part of the thorax

58 Shieldbugs have broad, flat bodies that look like leaves. The body is shaped like a shield carried by a medieval knight-in-armour.

◄ Shieldbugs stay on leaves of their own colour.

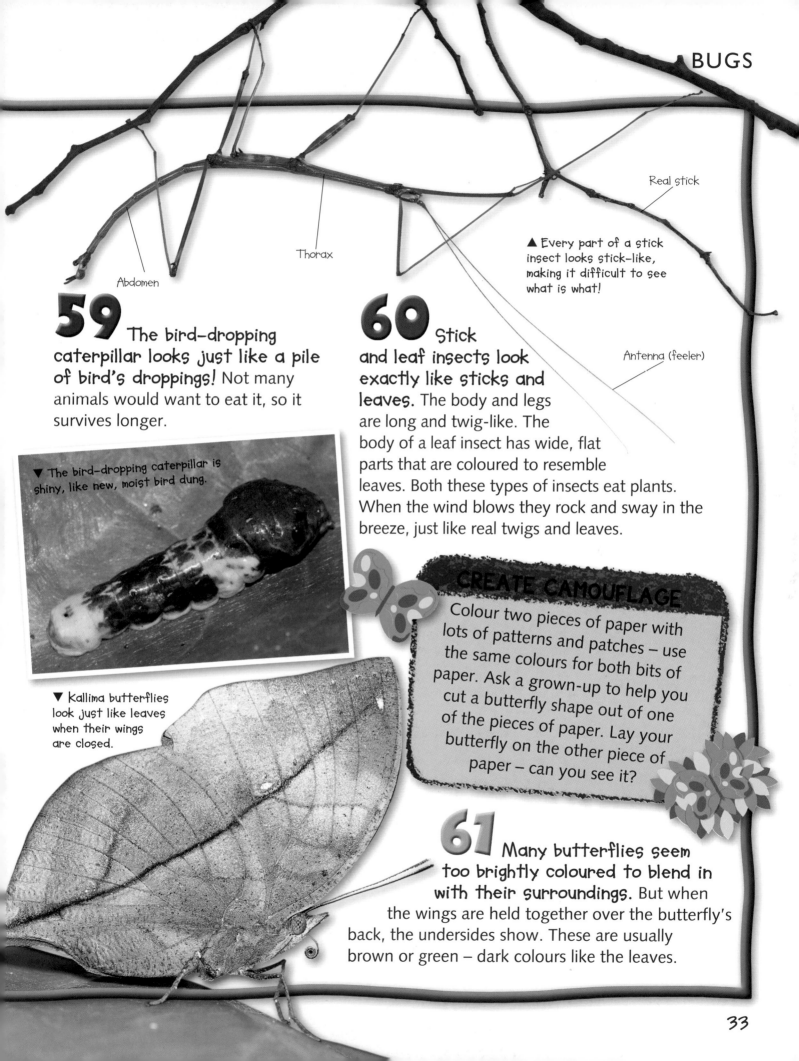

Real stick

Thorax

Abdomen

▲ Every part of a stick insect looks stick-like, making it difficult to see what is what!

Antenna (feeler)

59 The bird-dropping caterpillar looks just like a pile of bird's droppings! Not many animals would want to eat it, so it survives longer.

▼ The bird-dropping caterpillar is shiny, like new, moist bird dung.

60 Stick and leaf insects look exactly like sticks and leaves. The body and legs are long and twig-like. The body of a leaf insect has wide, flat parts that are coloured to resemble leaves. Both these types of insects eat plants. When the wind blows they rock and sway in the breeze, just like real twigs and leaves.

▼ Kallima butterflies look just like leaves when their wings are closed.

CREATE CAMOUFLAGE

Colour two pieces of paper with lots of patterns and patches – use the same colours for both bits of paper. Ask a grown-up to help you cut a butterfly shape out of one of the pieces of paper. Lay your butterfly on the other piece of paper – can you see it?

61 Many butterflies seem too brightly coloured to blend in with their surroundings. But when the wings are held together over the butterfly's back, the undersides show. These are usually brown or green – dark colours like the leaves.

Great pretenders

62 Some insects are shaped and coloured to look like other animals. This can make them seem stronger or more dangerous, even when they are not. Pretending to be another animal is known as mimicry.

◄ The harmless hoverfly looks just like a wasp. Like other mimics, it fools other animals into thinking it is more dangerous than it is.

Antennae sense prey

Large eyes

63 The animal pretending is called the mimic, the creature it looks like is called the model. Usually the model has a nasty sting, poisonous flesh or some other feature that protects it from attack.

◄ The ant beetle looks like the velvet ant, which has a painful sting.

Body pattern similar to velvet ant

64 The ant beetle resembles an ant. But it does not have a strong bite or sting like a real ant. The ant beetle enters the ants' nest and steals ant larvae to eat.

Monarch
butterfly (model)

Viceroy butterfly
(mimic)

65 The monarch butterfly has bright, bold colours on its wings. These warn other animals, such as birds and lizards, that its flesh tastes horrible and is poisonous. The viceroy butterfly looks very similar to the monarch, but its flesh is not distasteful.

▲ The viceroy butterfly is a mimic of the monarch butterfly.

66 The bee fly looks just like a bee. It has a hairy, striped body and can hover and hum like a bee, but it can't sting.

▶ The bee fly avoids predators by looking like a bee.

▲ Hornet moths have coloured wings, unlike real hornets.

67 The hornet moth is a mimic of the large type of wasp known as the hornet. A hornet has a very painful sting and few other creatures dare to try and eat it. The hornet moth is harmless, but few other creatures dare to eat it either.

QUIZ

1. Can the bee fly sting?
2. Which butterfly looks similar to the monarch butterfly?
3. Which insect does a hoverfly look like?

Answers:
1. No
2. Viceroy butterfly 3. Wasp

35

Stay or go?

68 The cold of winter or the dryness of drought mean hard times for most animals, including insects. One way to survive is to hibernate. Many insects find a safe, sheltered place and go to sleep because they are too cold to move. Butterflies crawl behind creepers and vines. Ladybirds cluster in thick bushes. Beetles dig into the soil or among tree roots. As the weather becomes warmer, they become active again.

▼ Ladybirds gather in jumbled piles for winter.

69 In North America, monarch butterflies fly south during autumn. They migrate to warmer areas and millions of them gather in winter roosts. Next spring they all fly north again to feed and breed.

70 Some insects migrate the wrong way! In Australia, bogong moths sometimes fly off in search of better conditions. Some keep on flying over the sea, fall into the water and die.

71 Some insects migrate only when they become too numerous. After a few years of good conditions in Africa, locusts (a type of large grasshopper) increase in number so much they form vast swarms. With so many locusts together, they eat all the food in a whole area then fly off to look for more. They eat massive areas of farm crops and people are left to starve.

▲ Some locust swarms are so vast, with billions of insects, they take several days to fly past.

Noisy neighbours

72 The tropical forest is warm and still — but far from quiet. Many insects are making chirps, buzzes, clicks, screeches, hums and other noises. Most are males, making their songs or calls to attract females at breeding time.

Large eye

Large wings

▶ Katydids, or bush crickets, have loud mating calls.

Chewing mouthparts

QUIZ

1. What noise does a cicada make?
2. How does the katydid make noise?
3. Why does a mole cricket dig a burrow?

Answers:
1. Buzzing sound 2. It rubs its wings together 3. To make its chirps louder

73 Some of the noisiest insects are cicadas, plant-eating bugs with large wings. The male cicada has two thin patches of body casing, called tymbals, one on either side of its abdomen (its rear body part). Tiny muscles pull in each patch, then let it go again, like clicking a tin lid in and out.

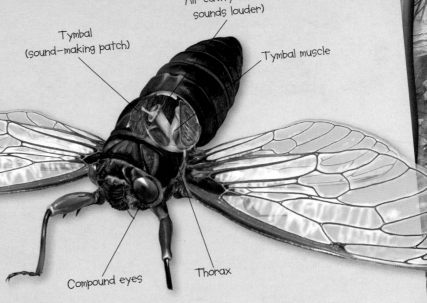

Tymbal (sound-making patch)

Air cavity (makes sounds louder)

Tymbal muscle

Thorax

Compound eyes

▶ A cicada's clicks are so fast, they merge into a buzzing sound, which can be heard one kilometre away.

74 The male mole cricket chirps like a katydid. It sits at the entrance to its burrow in the soil. The entrance is shaped like a loudspeaker, so it makes the chirps sound louder and travel further.

▶ The mole cricket's song is heard 2 kilometres away.

75 Like most other crickets, the male katydid chirps by rubbing its wings together. The bases of the wings near the body have hard, ridged strips like rows of pegs. These click past each other to make the chirping sound.

Meet the family!

76 **Are all minibeasts and bugs truly insects?** One way to tell is to count the legs. If a creature has six legs, it's an insect. If it has more legs or fewer, it is some other kind of animal. Leg-counting works only with adult creatures.

Single left and right wings

Hard forewing cases called elytra

▶ Flies are insects with six legs and one set of wings.

Flying hindwings folded up under elytra

▲ The cardinal beetle is an insect with six legs and two sets of wings.

▼ The red spider mite has eight legs, like its cousins, the spiders.

Furry body

Feelers and mouthparts

77 **Mites and ticks have eight legs, so they are not insects.** Ticks, and some mites, cling onto larger animals and suck their blood. Some mites are so small that a handful of soil may contain half a million of them. Mites and ticks belong to the group of animals with eight legs, called arachnids. Other arachnids are spiders and scorpions.

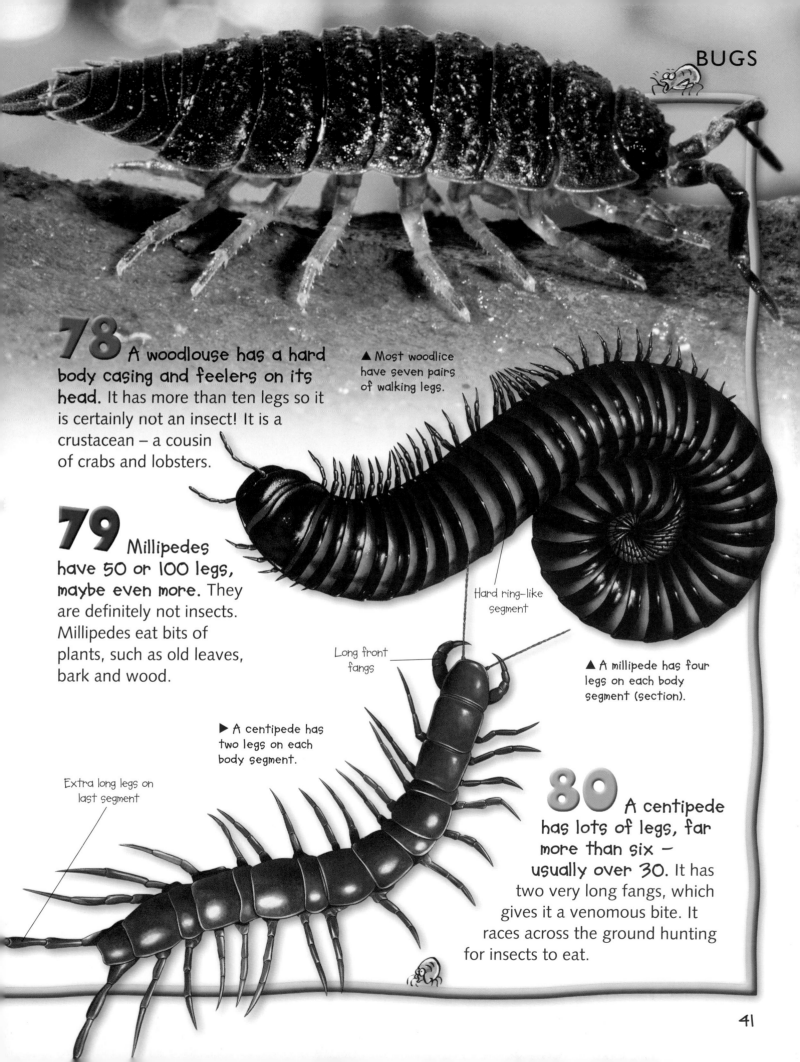

78 A woodlouse has a hard body casing and feelers on its head. It has more than ten legs so it is certainly not an insect! It is a crustacean – a cousin of crabs and lobsters.

▲ Most woodlice have seven pairs of walking legs.

79 Millipedes have 50 or 100 legs, maybe even more. They are definitely not insects. Millipedes eat bits of plants, such as old leaves, bark and wood.

Hard ring-like segment

Long front fangs

▲ A millipede has four legs on each body segment (section).

▶ A centipede has two legs on each body segment.

Extra long legs on last segment

80 A centipede has lots of legs, far more than six – usually over 30. It has two very long fangs, which gives it a venomous bite. It races across the ground hunting for insects to eat.

Silky spiders

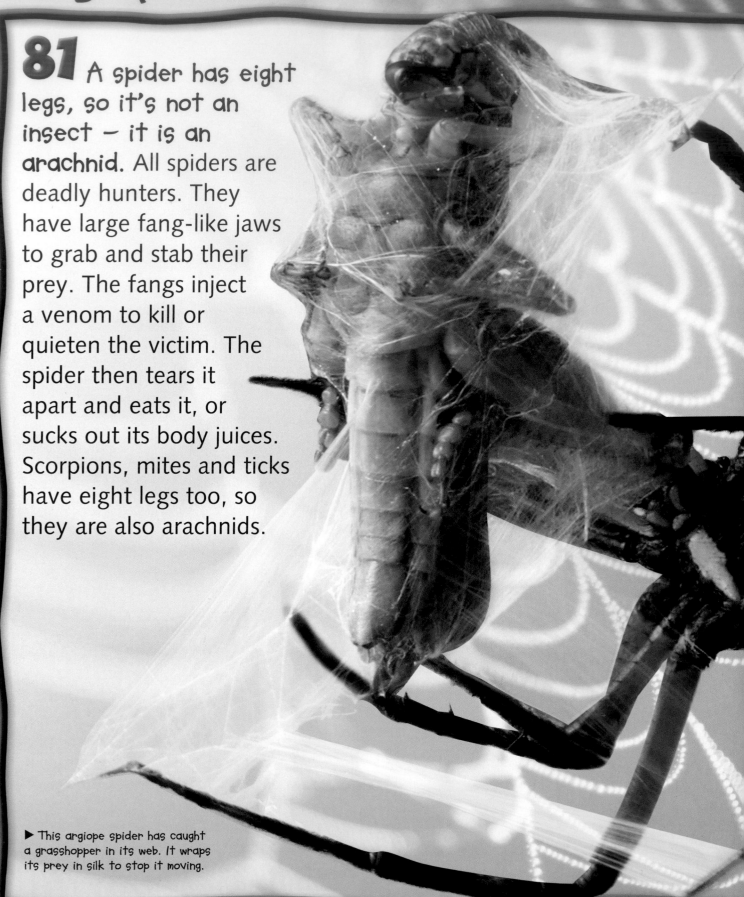

81 A spider has eight legs, so it's not an insect – it is an **arachnid**. All spiders are deadly hunters. They have large fang-like jaws to grab and stab their prey. The fangs inject a venom to kill or quieten the victim. The spider then tears it apart and eats it, or sucks out its body juices. Scorpions, mites and ticks have eight legs too, so they are also arachnids.

▶ This argiope spider has caught a grasshopper in its web. It wraps its prey in silk to stop it moving.

Several spinnerets produce silk

Spigots produce coarse silk for making webs

Spools produce fine silk for wrapping prey

Front legs wrap silk around prey

82 **All spiders can make thin, fine threads called silk.** These come out of spinnerets at the rear of the spider. About half of the 40,000 kinds of spiders make webs to catch prey. Some spiders make silk bags, called cocoons, to lay their eggs in or create protective 'nursery tents' for their young.

▶ The hardest part of building a web is getting the first thread in place. The spider needs a gust of wind to carry the thread across, so it sticks to a good spot.

① The first thread is horizontal

② The second thread makes a Y-shape

③ More strands, called radials, are added

④ A temporary spiral is put in place

⑤ The final spiral is built more carefully

83 **Some spiders use their silk threads in strange ways.** The spitting spider squirts sticky silk at its victim. The bolas spider creates a fishing line to catch insects flying past. The water spider makes a criss-cross sheet of silk to hold bubbles of air, which it needs in order to breathe underwater.

▼ The spitting spider spits a mixture of venom and 'glue' at its prey.

Inventive arachnids

84 Not all spiders catch their prey using webs. Wolf spiders are strong and have long legs. They can run fast and chase tiny prey such as beetles, caterpillars and slugs.

▶ The wolf spider stalks its prey, then makes a final rush at it.

▼ The crab spider watches for prey with its eight small eyes.

85 The crab spider looks like a small crab, with a wide, tubby body and curved legs. It usually sits on a flower that is the same colour as itself. It keeps very still so it is camouflaged. Small insects such as flies, beetles and bees come to the flower to gather food and the crab spider pounces on them.

86 Tarantulas are huge, hairy spiders. They live in tropical South America and Africa. Stretch out your hand and it still would not be as big as some of these giants! They are strong enough to catch small birds, mice, frogs and lizards.

Abdomen

87 The jumping spider is only 5–10 millimetres long, but it can leap more than 20 times this distance. It jumps onto tiny prey such as ants. The jumping spider's eyes are enormous for its small body, so it can see how far it needs to leap to land on its victim.

Safety line (trailing silk attached to a firm surface)

Cephalothorax (head–body section)

▲ The red-kneed tarantula can live for up to 40 years.

Prey is unaware of approaching spider

▲ The jumping spider has powerful rear legs.

Rear four legs adapted for leaping

88 The trapdoor spider lives in a burrow with a wedge-shaped door made from silk. The spider hides just behind this door. When it detects a small creature passing, it flips open the door and rushes out to grab its victim.

Deadly and dangerous

89 A scorpion has eight legs. Like a spider, it is an arachnid. Scorpions live in warm parts of the world. Some are at home in watery rainforests, others like hot deserts. The scorpion has large, crab-like pincers called pedipalps to grab its prey, and powerful jaws like scissors to chop it up.

90 The scorpion has a dangerous venomous sting at the tip of its tail. It can use this to paralyze or kill a victim. The scorpion may also wave its tail at enemies to warn them that unless they go away, it will sting them.

Stinger on last tail part

▶ This scorpion is attacking a grasshopper.

Pedipalp claws grab prey

91 The false scorpion looks like a scorpion with big pincers. It does not have a venomous sting in its tail – it does not even have a tail. It is tiny and could fit into this 'O'! It lives in soil and hunts even smaller creatures.

▶ False scorpions hunt tiny bugs, as small as a full stop.

92

A crab may seem an odd cousin for a spider or scorpion. But the horseshoe or king crab is very unusual. It has eight legs – so it's an arachnid. It also has a large domed shell and strong spiky tail. There were horseshoe crabs in the seas well before dinosaurs roamed the land.

▶ Horseshoe crabs come onto the shore at breeding time.

93

The sun spider or solifuge is another very fierce, spider-like hunter, although it has no venom. Most kinds live in deserts and are known as camel spiders.

94

Animals don't have to be big to be dangerous. These spiders are all very venomous and their bites can even kill people. This is why you should never mess about with spiders or poke your hands into holes or dark places!

The European black widow has up to 13 red patches on its abdomen

New Zealand's katipo is found along seashore dunes

The Australian redback has a body length of about 10 millimetres

QUIZ

1. Scorpions and spiders belong to which family group?

2. What does a scorpion use its tail for?

3. What is another name for a king crab?

Answers:
1. Arachnids 2. To paralyze the victim 3. Horseshoe crab

Friends and foes

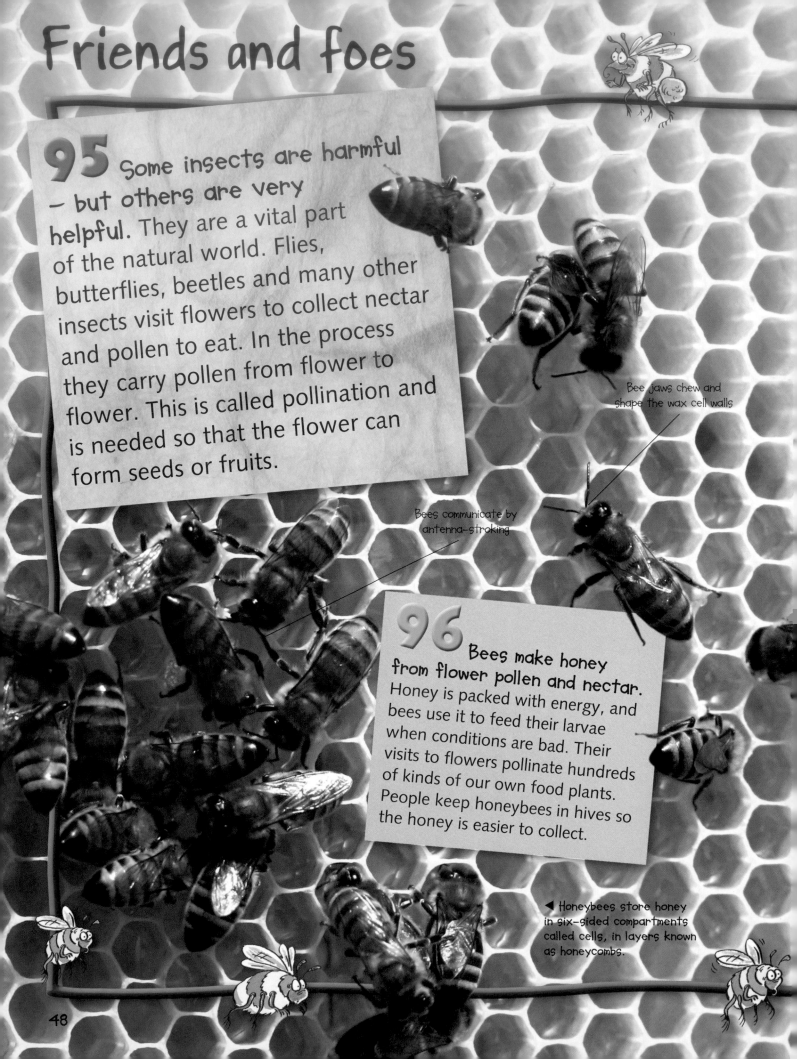

95 Some insects are harmful – but others are very helpful. They are a vital part of the natural world. Flies, butterflies, beetles and many other insects visit flowers to collect nectar and pollen to eat. In the process they carry pollen from flower to flower. This is called pollination and is needed so that the flower can form seeds or fruits.

Bee jaws chew and shape the wax cell walls

Bees communicate by antenna-stroking

96 Bees make honey from flower pollen and nectar. Honey is packed with energy, and bees use it to feed their larvae when conditions are bad. Their visits to flowers pollinate hundreds of kinds of our own food plants. People keep honeybees in hives so the honey is easier to collect.

◀ Honeybees store honey in six-sided compartments called cells, in layers known as honeycombs.

97 A few kinds of insects are among the most harmful creatures in the world. They do not attack and kill people directly, like tigers and crocodiles, but they do spread dangerous diseases, such as malaria.

98 Mosquitoes spread diseases by blood-sucking. Their blood-filled bodies are also food for a huge range of animals, from dragonflies and centipedes to frogs, small birds and shrews.

Abdomen held clear of skin

▶ A mosquito sucks blood from human skin.

Antennae detect skin warmth

Needle-like mouthparts in skin

▲ Spiders play a vital role in our ecosystem.

99 Spiders are very helpful to gardeners. They catch lots of insect pests, such as flies, in their webs.

100 Insects are so numerous and varied, they provide essential links to the food chains of almost every habitat. Countless small creatures eat insects who have eaten plants, then bigger animals eat the small creatures and so on. If insects disappeared, most other animal life would soon starve!

SHARKS

101 Sharks are meat-eating fish, and nearly all of them live in the sea. Many are active hunters and chase after their prey. Some lie in wait to grab their victims. Other kinds are scavengers, feasting on the dead bodies of animals such as whales and seals.

◄ Grey reef sharks are often seen in groups around coral islands, especially at night when they are most active. They are curious sharks that often swim close to divers, and near the water's surface.

The biggest sharks

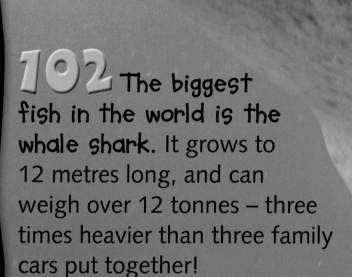

► The whale shark swims with its mouth wide open to filter krill from the water. Krill are usually 2 to 3 centimetres long. Millions of them, along with other small creatures, make up plankton.

102 The biggest fish in the world is the whale shark. It grows to 12 metres long, and can weigh over 12 tonnes – three times heavier than three family cars put together!

103 Whale sharks like cruising across the warm oceans. They swim up to 5000 kilometres in one year, but tend to visit the same areas at certain times of year, when their food is plentiful.

104 Despite the whale shark's huge size, it mostly eats tiny prey. It opens its enormous mouth, takes in a great gulp of water and squeezes it out through the gill slits on either side of its neck. Small animals such as krill and baby squid are trapped in the gills and then swallowed.

105 **Whale sharks may sleep for weeks.** It's thought that they sink to the seabed and lie there, hardly moving, for several weeks each year. This could help them to save energy when food is hard to come by.

▼ Ripple patterns on basking sharks are caused by sunlight shining through the waves onto the shark.

106 **Basking sharks are huge!** They are the second-biggest of all fish, reaching 10 metres in length and 6 tonnes in weight. Like whale sharks, basking sharks filter small animals and bits of food from the sea.

107 **Some sharks like to eat stinking, rotting flesh!** The Greenland shark can grow to a massive 7 metres in length. It feeds on all kinds of dead animal bodies, including whales, seals, dolphins, other sharks, squid and even drowned animals, such as reindeer.

▶ Greenland sharks rival great whites in size, weighing over one tonne. They swim slowly in the cold Arctic water.

Ancient sharks

▼ Sharks' basic body shapes and behaviour have hardly changed since they first appeared. The shark *Hybodus* lived about 160 million years ago in the Jurassic Period, during the Age of Dinosaurs.

108 The first sharks lived more than 350 million years ago. This was 120 million years before the dinosaurs lived on Earth. Dinosaurs died out around 65 million years ago but sharks survived. This means that sharks have ruled the seas for over twice as long as dinosaurs ruled the land!

▶ *Megalodon* was probably similar in appearance to today's great white. It was a top sea predator of its time and may have attacked marine mammals, such as this large whale.

109 Some prehistoric fish are known as 'spiny sharks'. This is because they had streamlined bodies like sharks, and sharp spikes on their fins and bellies. Their real name is acanthodians, and they lived in lakes and rivers 400 to 250 million years ago.

▲ A human diver looks tiny in comparison to the enormous *Megalodon* and its prey.

110 Some sharks are preserved in stone! Parts of sharks that died long ago have been preserved in rocks, as fossils. Most fossils are made of hard body parts, such as teeth and scales. The fossils show the size of the shark and even the kind of food it ate.

▶ Fossilized *Megalodon* teeth, being stone, are up to ten times heavier than they were in life.

111 The biggest shark in history was probably *Megalodon*. Its fossil teeth look like those of the great white shark, but they're twice as big. *Megalodon* could have been 15 or even 20 metres long – three times the size of today's great white. It lived about 20 to 2 million years ago and was a great hunter.

Megalodon

MAKE A MEGA MOUTH!

You will need:
black pen   big cardboard box   large pieces of white card   scissors   tape

1. Use the pen to draw a shark's mouth onto the box and cut it out.
2. Draw and cut out 20 teeth shapes from the white card.
3. Tape these inside the mouth. Draw on eyes. Now you can stare *Megalodon* in the face!

Super swimmers

112 Nearly all sharks have slim, streamlined bodies. This makes them fast swimmers – they slip through the water easily and travel at speed. One of the fastest sharks is the shortfin mako. It swims at more than 55 kilometres an hour – much faster than a champion human sprinter can run.

▲ The mako shark is slim and speedy, and races after prey such as mackerel, tuna and squid. It can leap more than 10 metres out of the water.

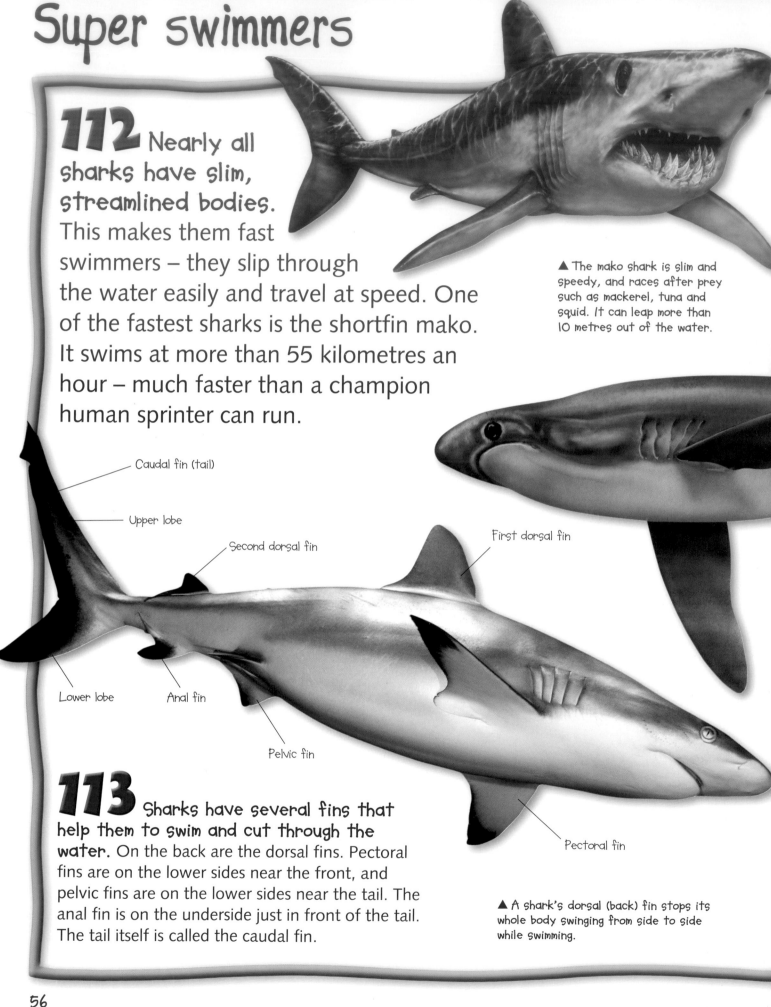

Caudal fin (tail)

Upper lobe

Second dorsal fin

First dorsal fin

Lower lobe

Anal fin

Pelvic fin

Pectoral fin

113 Sharks have several fins that help them to swim and cut through the water. On the back are the dorsal fins. Pectoral fins are on the lower sides near the front, and pelvic fins are on the lower sides near the tail. The anal fin is on the underside just in front of the tail. The tail itself is called the caudal fin.

▲ A shark's dorsal (back) fin stops its whole body swinging from side to side while swimming.

114 Some sharks have tails longer than their bodies. The common thresher shark is 6 metres long – and half of this is its tail. The thresher uses it to attack smaller fish, so it can eat them.

▼ The thresher shark thrashes its tail from side to side to stun small fish before swallowing them.

115 Shark tails have other uses, too. Some sharks smack the water's surface with their tails to frighten their prey. Others swish away sand or mud on the seabed to reveal any hidden creatures.

BREATHING UNDERWATER

1. Most sharks have five pairs of gills
2. Fine blood vessels allow oxygen to pass from the water to the blood
3. Heart pumps blood around the body

▶ A shark's gill chambers are in its neck region. Most have five gill slits on either side.

116 Like other fish, sharks breathe underwater using their gills. These are under the slits on either side of the head, and are filled with blood. Water flows in through the shark's mouth, over the gills and out through the slits. The gills take in oxygen from the water because sharks need oxygen to survive.

117 Most sharks swim all of the time so that water flows over their gills and they can breathe. However some can lie still and make the water flow over their gills by 'pumping' the muscles of their mouth and neck.

Making a meal

118 Tiger sharks are famous for trying to eat almost everything! Some of the items they swallow are not even food for them. They have even been known to eat tin cans and shoes!

119 Many predatory sharks will eat any suitable fishy prey they come across. This includes smaller sharks of other species, as well as their own. They may even eat their young.

▲ Tiger sharks usually feed at night, preferring to hunt alone.

120 Tiger sharks swim right up to the beach. Most sharks stay away from the shore in case they get stranded and die. But tiger sharks will come near to the shore, especially at night, to explore for food.

◄ The tiger shark can swim in water so shallow that it would hardly cover your knees. Here it can catch animals such as baby seals, and seabirds like this young albatross.

121 Where there is sudden plentiful food, like a dead whale, sharks gather and seem to go crazy. They bite and snap at almost anything – and occasionally even nip each other. This is called a feeding frenzy.

◀ A feeding frenzy is more organized than it looks – sharks rarely injure each other.

122 Most sharks prefer just a few types of food. One kind of bullhead shark likes to eat only sea urchins. However, if it gets very hungry, it will try other foods.

123 Not all sharks have sharp, pointed teeth. The Port Jackson shark has wide back teeth, like rounded pebbles. It uses these to crush the hard body cases of its favourite food – shellfish.

▶ The Port Jackson shark's front teeth are small and pointy, the rear ones are broad and strong.

Shark bodies

124 A shark has a skeleton but it is different to ours. The parts are made not of bone, but of a substance called cartilage. This substance is very strong and light, and also slightly bendy.

125 A shark's guts are about twice as long as its body. Swallowed food goes into the stomach, then along the intestine. This has a part called a spiral valve, found only in sharks and rays. It is shaped like a corkscrew and takes in nutrients from food.

Dorsal fin

Kidney

Intestines have a spiral valve

Backbone extends into tail

Stomach

126 Many sharks produce slime from their skin. It slides off the shark easily and helps the shark to swim faster. New slime is always being made quickly by the skin to replace the slime that flows away.

▲ The main parts of the skeleton are the skull, the ribs, the long backbone or vertebral column, and the fin spines.

127
Sharks have very tough skin covered with tiny, tooth-shaped points. These points are called denticles. In the bramble shark some of the denticles are much larger, forming sharp thorns and prickles for protection.

128
Shark skin can be useful. Through the ages it has been used by people as a strong material to make handbags, shoes, belts, cases, handle grips and even a special kind of sandpaper known as chagrin.

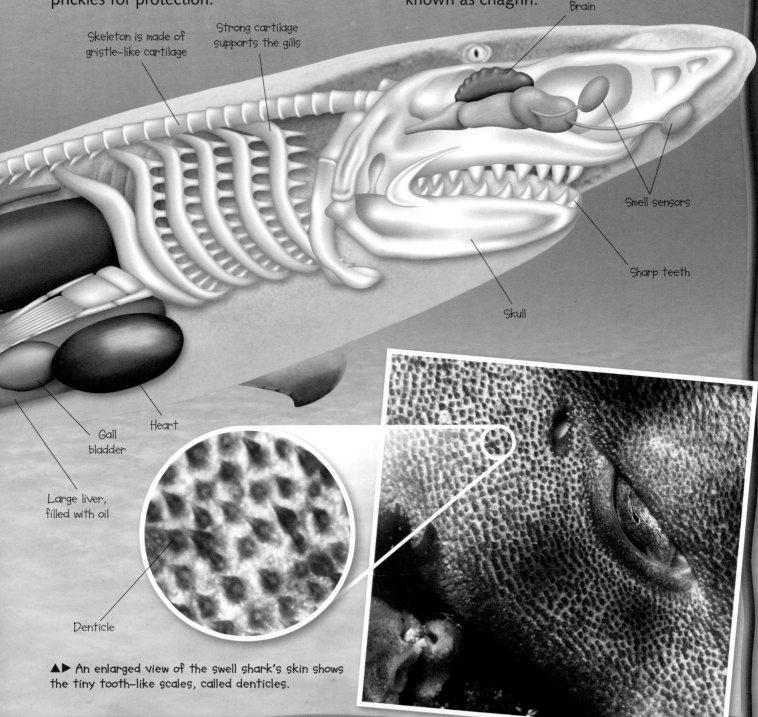

Skeleton is made of gristle-like cartilage

Strong cartilage supports the gills

Brain

Smell sensors

Sharp teeth

Skull

Gall bladder

Heart

Large liver, filled with oil

Denticle

▲▶ An enlarged view of the swell shark's skin shows the tiny tooth-like scales, called denticles.

Ultimate killer

129 The world's biggest hunting, or predatory, fish is the great white shark. It grows to 6 metres in length and can weigh more than one tonne. Great whites live around the world, mainly in warmer seas. They have a fearsome reputation.

▼ When attacking, the great white's final upwards rush, or charge, can carry it up to 5 metres above the surface.

130 The great white can raise its body temperature. It can make its body warmer than the surrounding water. This allows its muscles to work more quickly, so it can swim powerfully. It means the great white is partly warm-blooded, like humans.

131 Great whites let their victims bleed to death. They bite on their first charge then move off, leaving the victim with terrible wounds. When the injured prey is weak, the great white comes back to finish it off.

I DON'T BELIEVE IT!

A great white has about 300 razor-sharp teeth in its mouth. Its jaws open wide enough to swallow a whole seal in one gulp!

132 The teeth of the great white are up to 6 centimetres long. They are razor-sharp but slim, like blades, and they sometimes snap off. But new teeth are always growing just behind, ready to move forwards and replace the snapped-off teeth.

▼ The great white's upper teeth are triangular, the lower ones more pointed.

▼ Each tooth has jagged, saw-like edges called serrations.

134 The great white often attacks unseen from below. It surges up from the dark depths with tremendous power. It can smash into big prey such as a seal or a dolphin, and lift it right out of the water as it takes its first bite.

133 The great white 'saws' lumps from its victim. Each tooth has tiny sharp points along its edges. As the shark starts to feed, it bites hard and then shakes its head from side to side. The teeth work like rows of small saws to slice off a mouthful.

► When chasing prey or bait, great whites reach a top speed of over 40 kilometres an hour.

Strange sharks

135 Six-gill sharks have an extra pair of gills. This may be the number that ancient sharks had long ago. Six-gill sharks grow up to 5 metres long and eat various foods, from shellfish to dead dolphins.

Six pairs of curled gill slits

136 Some sharks have frills. The frilled shark has six pairs of wavy gill slits. It looks more like an eel than a shark, with a slim body 2 metres in length, and long frilly fins. It is dark brown in colour, lives in very deep waters and eats squid and octopus.

▲ Each tooth of the frilled shark has three needle-like points for grabbing soft-bodied prey.

▼ A saw shark may lose and re-grow as many as 30,000 teeth during its lifetime.

137 The saw shark has a 'saw' for a nose. Its long nose, or snout, is up to half its total length. The snout has teeth-like points sticking out from the sides. The shark uses its snout to dig around in sand and mud for prey.

138
The goblin shark looks very strange! Few examples have been found, so little is known about its lifestyle. It swims in very deep waters where there is no light – it may be able to detect its prey using an electro-sense.

▲ This young goblin shark has not yet grown its extra-long nose.

▼ The adult goblin shark's snout can be one-quarter of its total length. The jaws can move forwards, out of the mouth, to grab small fish and squid.

139
Lanternsharks can glow in the dark! They live in deep dark water and have glowing spots on their bodies, particularly around their mouths and along their sides. The spots may attract curious small creatures such as fish and squid, so the shark can snap them up.

▶ The lanternshark's tiny light-producing organs are called photophores.

Amazing senses

140 Most sharks have big eyes and can see well in the dark ocean. Many feed at night, or in deeper water where there's little light. This makes eyesight very important to the shark so that it can spot its prey. Some sharks have eyes that glow in the dark.

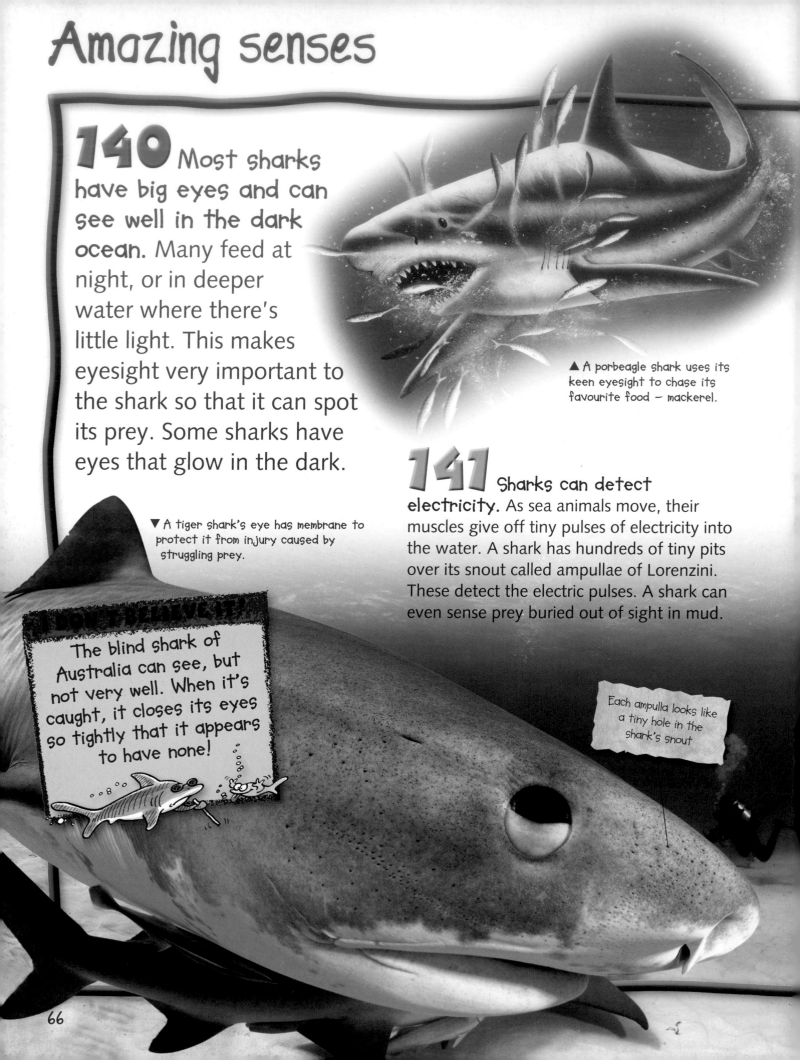

▲ A porbeagle shark uses its keen eyesight to chase its favourite food – mackerel.

▼ A tiger shark's eye has membrane to protect it from injury caused by struggling prey.

141 Sharks can detect electricity. As sea animals move, their muscles give off tiny pulses of electricity into the water. A shark has hundreds of tiny pits over its snout called ampullae of Lorenzini. These detect the electric pulses. A shark can even sense prey buried out of sight in mud.

Each ampulla looks like a tiny hole in the shark's snout

142 Sharks can hear divers breathing! They detect the sound of air bubbles coming from the scuba-divers' mouths. Hearing is not a shark's best sense – its ear openings are tiny.

▼ Sharks detect a diver by sight, sound and feeling ripples – the dive suit reduces smell and electro-sensing.

143 Sharks have an amazing sense of smell. It is their best long-range sense. From several kilometres away, they can detect blood or body fluids from a wounded animal. A shark 'sniffs' water into the nostrils on its snout, just like a human draws air into his or her nose.

144 Sharks often test-taste their food before eating. They will take a small nibble of an unfamiliar food to check that it's suitable to eat. Some sharks have taste buds on their snouts, so they can detect the flavour of food by rubbing their noses on it.

145 Like us, sharks can feel things that touch their skin. They also have an extra sense organ called the lateral line. This is a long tube running down each side of a shark's body, under its skin. Ripples in the water pass into the lateral line through tiny holes in the skin. Hairs inside the lateral line sense the ripples and send signals to the brain.

◄ The lateral line runs along the side of the body from head to tail base.

Lateral line

67

Hammers for heads

146 The hammerhead shark is named after the strange shape of its head. Experts suggest several reasons for this – one is that the head is shaped like the wings of a plane. As the shark swims, water flowing over its head helps to keep its front end lifted up, rather than nose-diving.

Large hammer-shaped head with eyes and nostrils at either end

Triangular, serrated teeth

▶ The hammerhead's mouth is relatively small compared to the width of its head – but still deadly for small prey.

147 The hammer-shaped head may improve the shark's senses. The nostrils are at each end of the 'hammer'. Smells drifting from the side reach one nostril well before the other. By swinging its head from side to side, the hammerhead can pinpoint the direction of a smell more quickly.

QUIZ

Why might hammerheads have hammer-shaped heads?

1. To break apart rocks to get at prey behind them.
2. To help sense the direction of smells in the water.
3. To smash open windows in shipwrecks.

148 The great hammerhead is one of the biggest predatory sharks, growing to 6 metres long. There are another eight kinds of hammerhead shark, including the scalloped hammerhead and the bonnet-head.

Answer: 2

149

Hammerheads are among the most dangerous sharks. They have been known to attack people, although their usual food includes fish, squid, crabs and shellfish. They eat stingrays too and don't seem to be affected by the painful sting.

Tall dorsal fin

Much larger upper tail lobe than lower lobe

► A bonnet-head shark swallows a ray it has just found part-buried in seabed sand.

150

Most sharks live alone, but hammerheads like a crowd. They gather together in huge groups called schools at certain times of the year, probably to breed.

Big mouth

151 The megamouth shark was discovered in 1976 near Hawaii in the Pacific Ocean. An American research ship hauled in its parachute-like anchor to find a strange shark tangled in it.

▼ The megamouth's huge jaws are right at the front of its body, not slung under the head as in most sharks.

152 Megamouths open their mouths as they swim through shoals of krill. The prey get trapped inside the shark's mouth and then swallowed. The megamouth is not really an active hunter. It is a slow-swimming filter-feeder, like the whale and basking shark.

153 Megamouths go up and down every day. They rise near to the surface at dusk in order to feed during the night. At dawn they sink to deeper waters and spend the day in the dark, more than 200 metres down.

The loose skin and floppy fins show that the megamouth is a slow swimmer

154 Megamouths are scattered around the world. They have been caught in all the tropical oceans, especially in the Western Pacific and Indian oceans. Only about 50 have been found since its discovery. It may be that there have never been many megamouths in the world.

▲ Although the megamouth is rare, it can live worldwide. Each shark icon shows where a specimen has been found.

155 The megamouth has a massive mouth more than 1.3 metres wide. Its soft, flabby body is about 5 metres long. In the summer when it has been feeding well, it can weigh more than one tonne.

156 Scientists believe that there may be more types of shark as yet undiscovered. Sometimes the badly-rotted bodies of strange sharks are washed up onto beaches. But the remains are often too decayed to be identified.

Getting up close

▼ The whale shark has little to fear from humans, so divers can usually approach, and even grab a ride by holding the dorsal fin.

157 Some small types of shark are fairly safe and people can swim near them with care. In some tourist areas, people can even feed sharks. The sharks seem to become trained to accept food from divers.

158 Some sharks, however, are dangerous to swim with. Although the cookie-cutter shark is only 50 centimetres long, it has a large mouth and big, sharp teeth. This shark attacks targets much larger than itself, biting out small patches of skin and flesh, before racing away. It even snaps at humans – the first recorded case was in 2009. Victims are left with neat round holes in their bodies.

▶ The circular bite mark made by a cookie-cutter shark can be clearly seen on this spinner dolphin as it leaps through the waves.

QUIZ

Which sharks aren't usually dangerous to people?

1. White-tip reef shark
2. Great white
3. Nurse shark
4. Thresher
5. Tiger shark

Answer: 1, 3, 4

159 Some sharks get used to accepting food from people. This means that they get out of the habit of hunting. When the people are no longer around, the sharks start to starve.

160 Feeding and touching sharks is now banned in some places. Sometimes a shark snatches and swallows the food while it's still in a bag or net. This could give the shark bad stomach-ache, or even kill it. Also, touching sharks and other fish can damage their skin, scales and layers of body slime.

▶ A shark cage allows divers to get a close up view of a great white. An encounter like this would be incredibly dangerous without it.

In the family

161 Sharks have close relations that also have skeletons made of cartilage rather than bone. Other kinds of cartilaginous fish include skates and rays, and the chimaera.

▼ The huge manta ray has two fleshy 'lobes' on its head that guide water into its mouth. The manta then filters the water to find food.

162 Skates and rays are flat fish, but not flatfish. True flatfish, such as plaice, have bony skeletons and lie on their left or right side. Skates and rays have very wide bodies with flattened upper and lower surfaces, and long narrow tails.

THE FLYING RAY

You will need:

scissors   stiff paper   coloured pens
sticky tape   drinking straw
modelling clay

1. Cut out a ray shape from paper and colour it brightly. Fold it along the middle so the 'wings' angle upwards.
2. Stick the straw along the underside, so part sticks out as a 'tail'. Add a blob of modelling clay to one end.
3. Launch your 'flying ray' into the air. Adjust the tail weight until it glides smoothly.

163 A ray or skate 'flies' through the water. The sides of its body extend out like wings. The 'wings' push the water backwards, and so the ray or skate swims forwards. Unlike sharks and other fish, the ray's tail is rarely used for swimming.

164 The biggest rays are mantas.

They measure up to 7 metres across and weigh nearly 2 tonnes. Manta rays have huge mouths and feed like whale sharks by filtering small creatures from the water. Despite their great size, mantas can leap clear of the surface and crash back with a huge splash.

165 Stingrays have sharp spines on their long tails.

They use them like daggers to jab poison into enemies or victims. Some stingrays live in lakes and rivers.

▶ The blue-spotted stingray grows to about 35 centimetres across.

Pale undersides with blotches

Short tail without sting

Large pectoral fins

166 Sawfish are different from saw-sharks.

A sawfish is shaped like a shark, but it is a type of ray with a long snout edged by pointed teeth. A sawfish has gill slits on the bottom of its body, rather than on the side.

Edged with sharp 'teeth'

Gilll slits

Long, saw-like snout

▲ The sawfish uses its saw to catch prey, either by swiping at shoals of fish, or sifting through sand to find crustaceans.

Meeting and mating

167 Female sharks need male sharks of the same species to produce young. When a male and a female get together, they mate. Then the female produces offspring. Some types of shark lay eggs, while others give birth to live young.

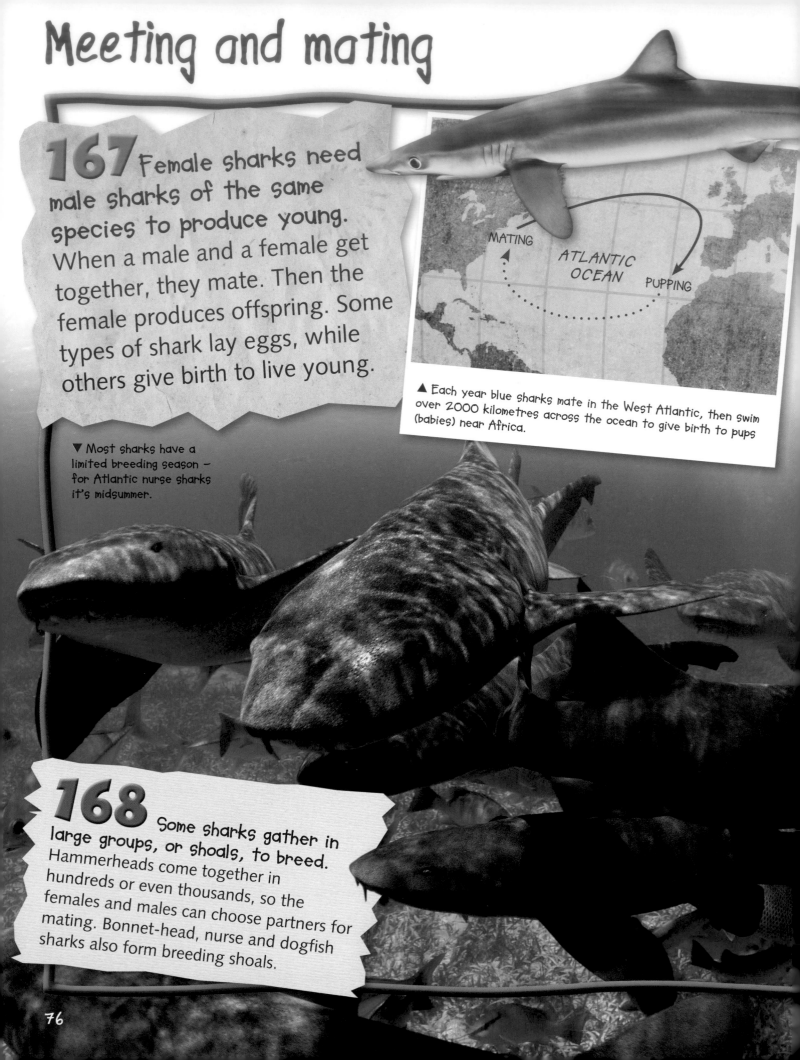

MATING

ATLANTIC OCEAN

PUPPING

▲ Each year blue sharks mate in the West Atlantic, then swim over 2000 kilometres across the ocean to give birth to pups (babies) near Africa.

▼ Most sharks have a limited breeding season – for Atlantic nurse sharks it's midsummer.

168 Some sharks gather in large groups, or shoals, to breed. Hammerheads come together in hundreds or even thousands, so the females and males can choose partners for mating. Bonnet-head, nurse and dogfish sharks also form breeding shoals.

▲ Male white-tip reef sharks rest in the shallows, waiting for scents called pheromones to drift through the water, which tells them that females are nearby.

169 Sharks have a complicated way of getting together. They give off scents into the water to attract a partner. Then the two rub one another, wind their bodies around each other, and sometimes even bite the other. The male may hold the female using his claspers, which are two long parts on his underside.

170 Some sharks don't breed very often. This can cause problems, especially when people catch too many of them. The sharks cannot breed fast enough to keep up their numbers, and they become rare.

Eggs and babies

171 Some mother sharks lay eggs. Each egg has a strong case with a developing baby shark, called an embryo, inside. The case has long threads, which stick to seaweed or rocks. Look out for empty egg cases on beaches. They are known as 'mermaids' purses'.

I DON'T BELIEVE IT!

As the young of the sand tiger shark develop inside their mother, the bigger ones feed on the smaller ones!

▼ A baby catshark develops slowly in its protective case. At 50 days it is smaller than its store of food, the yolk. It gradually develops and finally hatches eight months later.

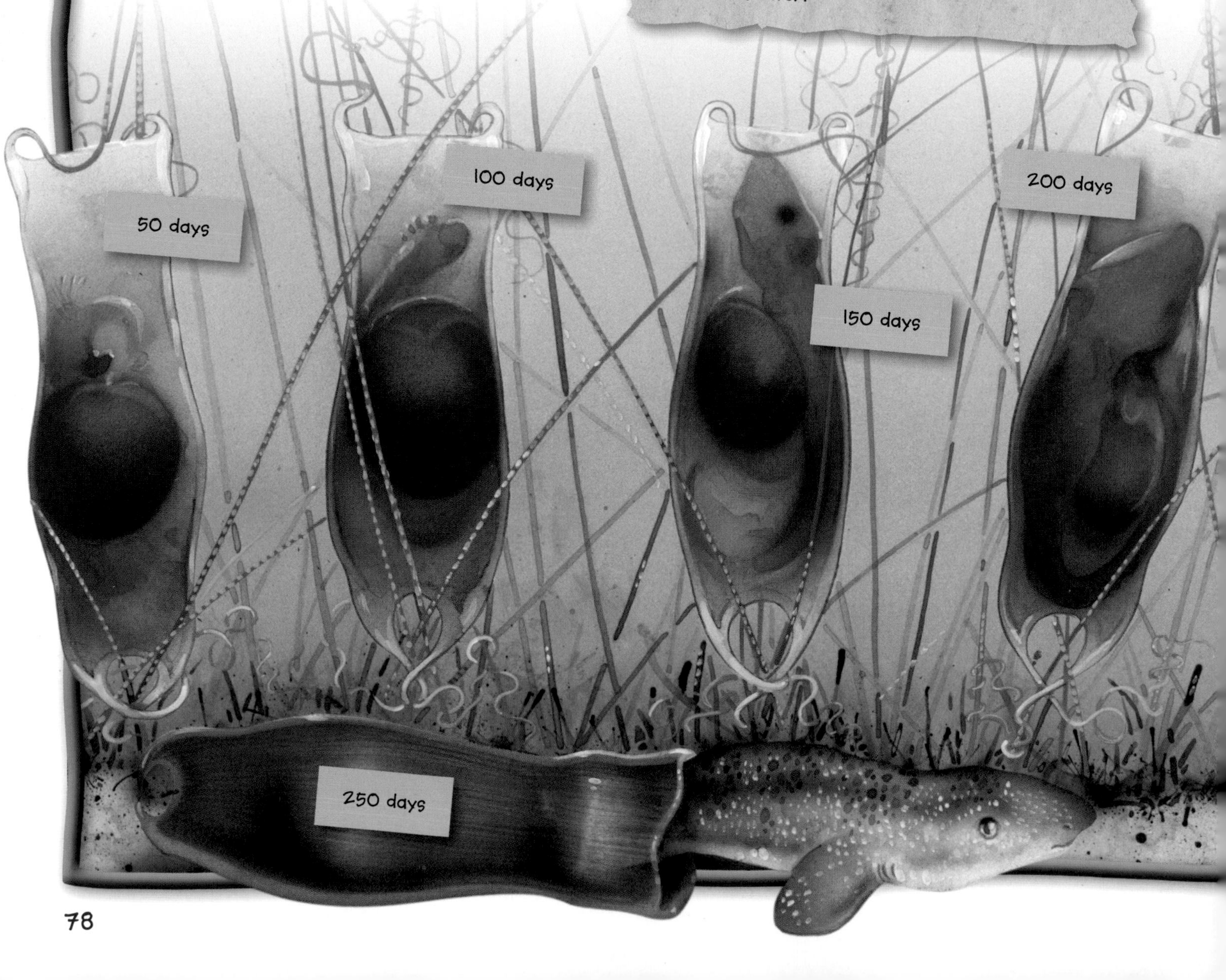

100 days

50 days

200 days

150 days

250 days

▶ Shark pups, like this newborn baby lemon shark, receive no parental care and must survive by themselves from birth.

172
Some mother sharks give birth to live baby sharks, known as pups. The basking and hammerhead shark do this. The pups have to look after themselves straight away.

▲ This just-hatched bamboo shark pup, about 30 centimetres long, still has some yolk as food.

173
Some sharks have hundreds of babies at once. The whale shark may give birth to as many as 300 pups, each about 60 centimetres long.

174
Many young sharks die. The mothers lay eggs or give birth in sheltered places such as bays, inlets and reefs, to try and keep the pups safe. But they are easy prey for hunters, such as dolphins, barracudas, sea lions and other sharks.

◀ The egg cases of the Port Jackson shark are spiral-shaped. The mother picks up each egg in her mouth and wedges it into a safe place, such as under a rock.

Hide and seek

175 Some sharks blend into their surroundings. This is called camouflage. The wobbegong has a lumpy body with blotches and frills that look just like rocks and seaweed. It waits for a fish to swim past, then opens its huge mouth to grab the victim.

▶ The mottled pattern, lumpy skin and frilly mouth of the wobbegong means it is difficult to spot from above, as it lies silently on the seabed.

176 A young zebra shark's stripes may camouflage it as it lies on ridges of mud or sand formed by water currents. The stripes also blend in with the shadows on the seabed formed by ripples on the surface above. As the shark grows, its stripes split into spots.

▼ This adult zebra shark's spots were once connected to form stripes.

▲ The flattened body of the angel shark looks like a low hump or rise in the sandy seabed. The shark must stay still to make the most of its camouflage.

177
Angel sharks have wide, flat bodies the same colour as sand. They blend perfectly into the sandy seabed as they lie in wait for prey. They are called 'angel' sharks because their fins spread wide like an angel's wings.

178
Even in the open ocean, sharks can be hard to spot. This is because of the way they are coloured, known as countershading. The shark's back is darker while its underside is lighter. Seen from above the dark back blends in with the gloom of deeper water below. Seen from below the pale belly merges with the brighter water's surface and sky above.

▲ A side view of this grey reef shark shows countershading — a darker back and a lighter underside.

Making friends

179 Some fish enter a shark's mouth – and live! These small, brightly coloured fish are called cleaner wrasse. The shark allows them to nibble off bits of skin, scales and pests such as sea leeches and barnacles from its body, gills, mouth and teeth. The shark gets cleaned, and the cleaner fish have a good meal. This is an example of 'symbiosis'.

▼ This lemon shark is waiting patiently as striped cleaner wrasse move in between its teeth, cleaning as they go.

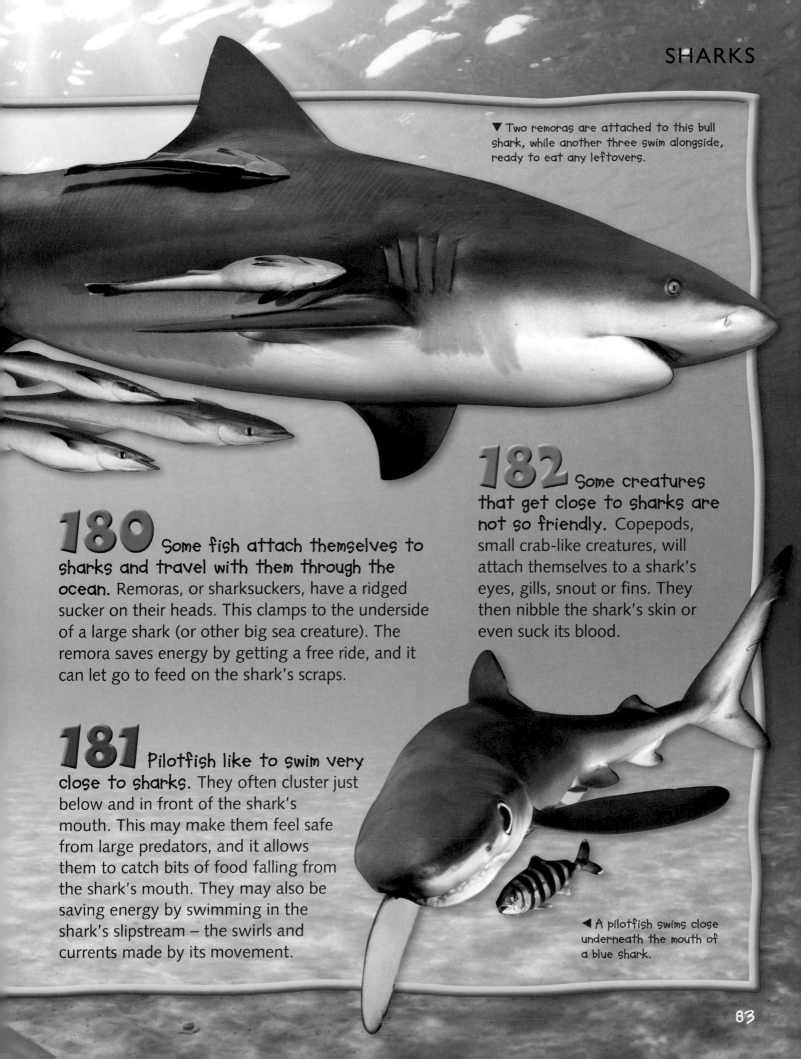

▼ Two remoras are attached to this bull shark, while another three swim alongside, ready to eat any leftovers.

180 Some fish attach themselves to sharks and travel with them through the ocean. Remoras, or sharksuckers, have a ridged sucker on their heads. This clamps to the underside of a large shark (or other big sea creature). The remora saves energy by getting a free ride, and it can let go to feed on the shark's scraps.

181 Pilotfish like to swim very close to sharks. They often cluster just below and in front of the shark's mouth. This may make them feel safe from large predators, and it allows them to catch bits of food falling from the shark's mouth. They may also be saving energy by swimming in the shark's slipstream – the swirls and currents made by its movement.

182 Some creatures that get close to sharks are not so friendly. Copepods, small crab-like creatures, will attach themselves to a shark's eyes, gills, snout or fins. They then nibble the shark's skin or even suck its blood.

◄ A pilotfish swims close underneath the mouth of a blue shark.

On the move

183 There are about 470 kinds of sharks, but only a few leave the sea and swim into the fresh water of rivers. One is the bull shark, which travels hundreds of kilometres up rivers, especially in South America.

184 Sharks may have a built-in compass. People use magnetic compasses to find their way across the seas or remote lands. The compass detects the natural magnetism of the Earth and points north-south. Sharks may be able to detect the Earth's magnetism too, using tiny parts of their bodies.

185 The most widespread sharks are blue sharks. They are found in almost every part of every ocean, except the icy polar seas. In the Atlantic Ocean, they travel from the Caribbean to Western Europe, down to Africa, and back to the Caribbean – 6000 kilometres in one year!

▶ Bull sharks have been known to attack people fishing, washing or boating in lakes. These bull sharks are in the Bahamas, very close to the shore.

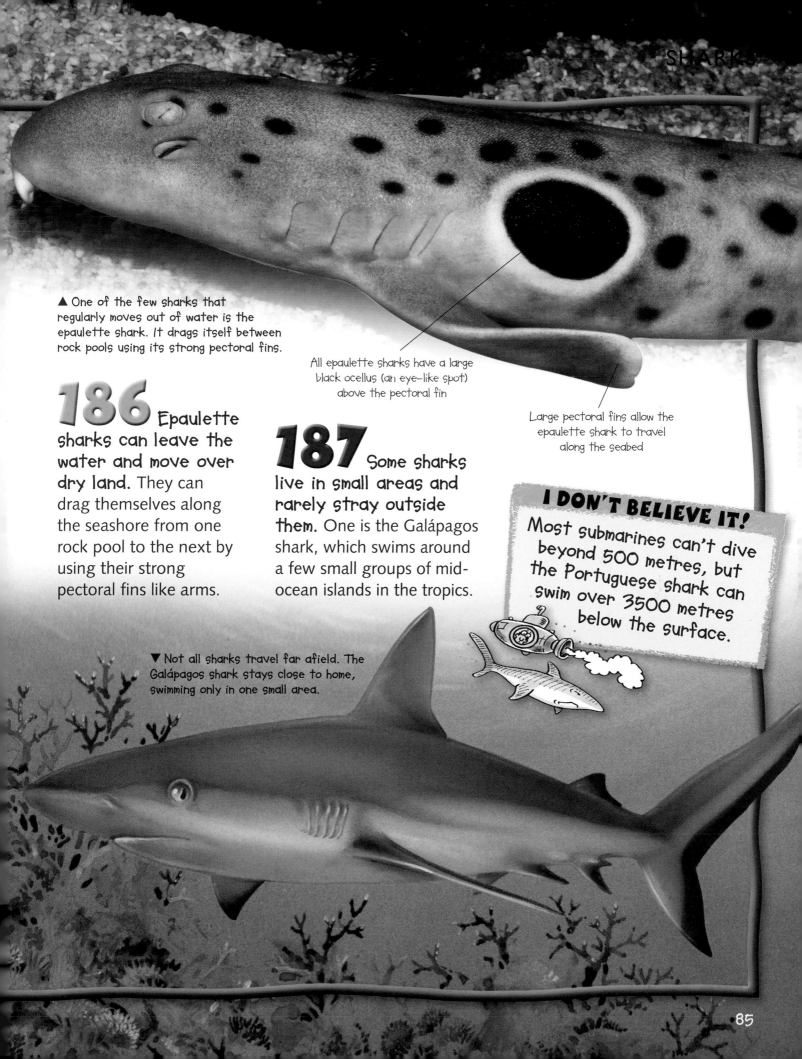

▲ One of the few sharks that regularly moves out of water is the epaulette shark. It drags itself between rock pools using its strong pectoral fins.

All epaulette sharks have a large black ocellus (an eye-like spot) above the pectoral fin

Large pectoral fins allow the epaulette shark to travel along the seabed

186 Epaulette sharks can leave the water and move over dry land. They can drag themselves along the seashore from one rock pool to the next by using their strong pectoral fins like arms.

187 Some sharks live in small areas and rarely stray outside them. One is the Galápagos shark, which swims around a few small groups of mid-ocean islands in the tropics.

I DON'T BELIEVE IT!
Most submarines can't dive beyond 500 metres, but the Portuguese shark can swim over 3500 metres below the surface.

▼ Not all sharks travel far afield. The Galápagos shark stays close to home, swimming only in one small area.

Science and sharks

188 Scientists study how sharks live, behave and travel. Small radio-transmitter trackers can be attached to big sharks and the radio signals show where the shark roams. Scientists attach little plastic tags with letters and numbers to the fins of smaller sharks. If the shark is caught again, its code can be traced.

189 Sharks show us problems in the oceans. In some areas, sharks have disappeared for no obvious reason. This might suggest chemicals and pollution in the water, which upset the balance of nature. The chemicals could affect the sharks themselves, making them unwell so that they travel away. Or the pollution could affect the sharks' prey, meaning they have to hunt elsewhere for food.

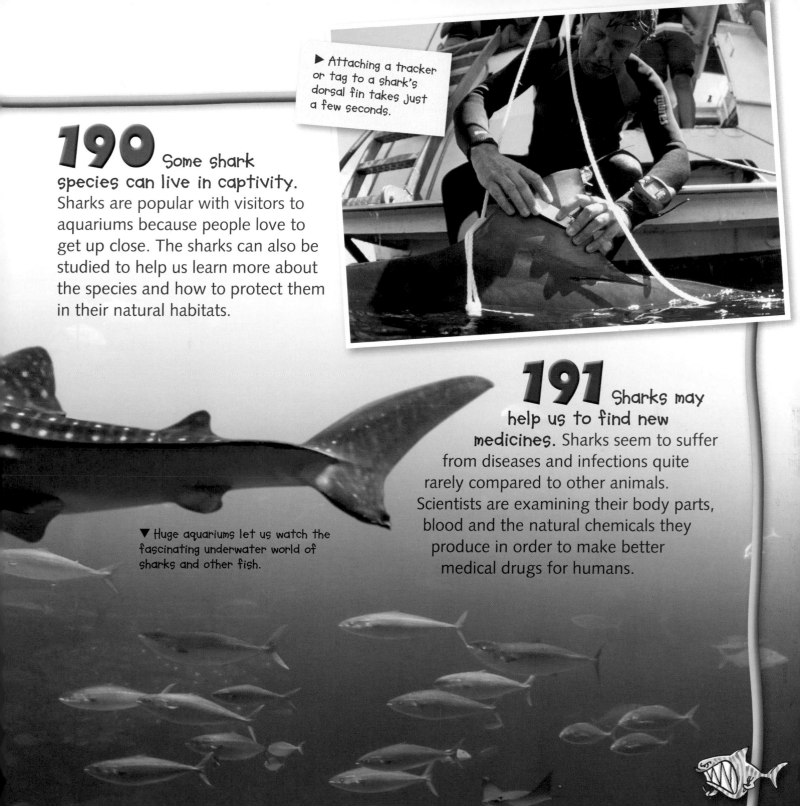

► Attaching a tracker or tag to a shark's dorsal fin takes just a few seconds.

190

Some shark species can live in captivity. Sharks are popular with visitors to aquariums because people love to get up close. The sharks can also be studied to help us learn more about the species and how to protect them in their natural habitats.

▼ Huge aquariums let us watch the fascinating underwater world of sharks and other fish.

191

Sharks may help us to find new medicines. Sharks seem to suffer from diseases and infections quite rarely compared to other animals. Scientists are examining their body parts, blood and the natural chemicals they produce in order to make better medical drugs for humans.

Watch out!

192 The most dangerous sharks include the great white, tiger and bull sharks. However, a shark that attacks a person might not be properly identified. Attacks are quick and the shark is soon gone. Some attacks blamed on great whites might have been made by bull sharks instead.

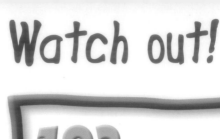

▼ Seeing a great white shark's fin may cause swimmers to panic and splash. If the shark confuses the swimmer for prey it may attack.

▶ From below, a surfboard's shape is similar to a seal or a turtle, which may be the reason why large hunting sharks sometimes attack surfers.

193 Certain places around the world are known for shark attacks. These include the east coast of North America, the west coast of Africa and around Southeast Asia and Australia. This is partly because these places are popular with swimmers and surfers.

194 Most shark attacks aren't fatal. A shark may 'test-bite' a person before realizing they aren't its normal prey. The victim may be injured, but not killed. Sharks will usually only attack people if they are hungry, or they may mistake humans for their normal prey.

▶ A chain-metal shark suit protects this diver as a blue shark 'mouths' or test-tastes.

▶ Safe from attack beyond the rope, tourists watch and learn as trained blacktip reef sharks are fed.

195 The dangers of shark attacks can be reduced in many ways. Examples include shark barriers or nets around the beach, patrols by boats and planes, lookout towers, and only swimming in protected areas.

196 Sharks are not the world's most dangerous animals. Each year, many more people are killed by poisonous snakes, tigers, elephants, hippos and crocodiles.

Save our sharks

197 Some shark species have become very rare. There are lots of reasons for this – pollution, hunting by people who think that all sharks are dangerous, sports angling where people use rods and lines to hook sharks, catching sharks for their meat, and catching sharks by accident in nets meant for other fish.

QUIZ

Put these sharks in order of size, starting with the smallest to the biggest:

A. Great white

B. Lesser spotted dogfish

C. Nurse shark

D. Frilled shark

Answers:
1. B 2. D
3. C 4. A

▼ By getting very close to sharks, and studying their behaviour, experts can help the conservation effort.

◄ Disguarded fishing nets can trap sharks, such as this young hammerhead.

198 Live sharks can be worth more than dead ones. People pay to see sharks in their natural habitats, viewing from glass-bottomed boats or underwater tunnels. In ecotourism, people experience nature without damaging it, and profits are used to help animals, plants and their habitats.

199 Sharks can be made into many foods, including shark fin soup. Many other shark parts are eaten or used by people around the world, including the flesh as shark steaks, and the liver and other body parts in various oils, cosmetics and health foods. Sometimes, it's not obvious because names are changed. Meat from a dogfish shark may be sold as 'rock salmon' or 'rock cod'.

▲ Shark oil is said to improve health, but there is no scientific proof.

200 Some sharks need our help, or they will die out forever. One of the best ways is to set aside huge areas of sea and coast as marine nature reserves or sanctuaries. Here all the animals can be protected from harm.

201 Reptiles and amphibians are cold-blooded animals. This means that they need the Sun's heat to warm them up. Reptiles spend much of their time on land, but most amphibians live in or around water.

Ear

Dry, scaly skin

Sharp claws

▶ The skin of an amphibian is smooth and moist. Most amphibians, such as this frog, have long hind legs that are ideal for jumping.

Smooth, moist skin

Large eyes

Long hind legs

Long toes

Four legs

Long tail

Four legs

◀ Reptiles, such as this lizard, have dry, scaly skin and are often colourful creatures. Not all reptiles have legs, but if they do, their legs are on the sides of their bodies.

Scales and slime

202 Reptiles and amphibians can be divided into smaller groups. There are four kinds of reptiles – snakes, lizards and amphisbaenians, the crocodile family, tortoises and turtles, and the tuatara. Amphibians are split into frogs and toads, newts and salamanders, and caecilians.

203 Reptiles do a lot of sunbathing! Sitting in the sun is called basking – reptiles bask to warm themselves with the Sun's heat so they can move. When it gets cold, at night or during a cold season, reptiles might hibernate, which is a type of deep sleep.

▶ Blue-collared lizards may bask for many hours at a time.

Reptile family

Over half of all reptiles are lizards – there are nearly 5000 species.

Amphisbaenians, or worm lizards, are burrowing reptiles that live underground.

Tuataras are rare, ancient and unusual reptiles from New Zealand.

Snakes are the second largest group of reptiles.

Crocodiles, alligators, gharials and caimans are predators with sharp teeth.

Turtles and tortoises have hard shells that protect them from predators.

204 Most reptiles have dry, scaly, waterproof skin. This stops their bodies from drying out. The scales are made of keratin and may form thick, tough plates. Human nails are made of the same material.

Amphibian family

Newts have slender bodies and long tails.

Frogs have smooth skin and long legs for jumping.

Toads often have warty skin and crawl or walk.

Salamanders have tails and they usually have bright markings.

Caecilians are burrowing animals without legs.

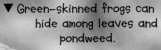
▼ Green—skinned frogs can hide among leaves and pondweed.

QUIZ

1. Why do reptiles bask?
2. How do most amphibians breathe?
3. How do reptiles breathe?

Answers:
1. To warm themselves with the Sun's heat so they can move 2. Through their skin and with their lungs 3. With their lungs

205 **Amphibians have skin that is moist, smooth and soft.** Oxygen can pass easily through their skin, which is important because most adult amphibians breathe through their skin as well as with their lungs. Reptiles breathe only with their lungs.

206 **Amphibians' skin is kept moist by special glands just under the surface.** These glands produce a sticky substance called mucus. Many amphibians also keep their skin moist by making sure that they are never far away from water.

207 **Some amphibians have no lungs.** Humans breathe with their lungs to get oxygen from the air and breathe out carbon dioxide. Most amphibians breathe through their skin and lungs, but lungless salamanders breathe only through their skin and the lining of the mouth.

Sun worshippers

208 Most reptiles live in warm or hot habitats. Many are found in dry, burning-hot places such as deserts and dry grassland. They have various clever ways of surviving in these harsh conditions.

▼ Thorny devils are Australian reptiles. When it rains, water trickles along a thorny devil's back, towards its mouth!

209 Even reptiles can get too hot sometimes! When this happens, they hide in the shade of a rock or bury themselves in the sand. Some escape the heat by being nocturnal – coming out mostly at night.

210 Reptiles need very little food and water. That means they can survive in places where there are not many plants or animals to eat, such as deserts. Their thick skin has an important job to do – it stops too much water from escaping from their bodies.

▲ A spadefoot toad has strong, clawed feet for digging.

211 Reptiles need a certain level of warmth to survive. This is why there are no reptiles in very cold places, such as at the North and South Poles, or at the very tops of mountains.

212 Like reptiles, many amphibians live in very hot places. Sometimes it can get too hot and dry for them. The spadefoot toad from Europe, Asia and North America buries itself in the sand to escape the heat and dryness.

I DON'T BELIEVE IT!

The sand lizard of the African Namib Desert performs strange dances. When it gets too hot, it may lift its legs up and down off the burning sand, or lie on its stomach and raise all its legs at once!

Cooler customers

213 Many amphibians are common in cooler, damper parts of the world. Amphibians like wet places. Most mate and lay their eggs in water.

▶ Frogs can hide from strong sunlight by resting in trees or under plants.

214 As spring arrives, amphibians come out of hiding. The warmer weather sees many amphibians returning to the pond or stream where they were born. This may mean a very long journey through towns or over busy roads.

◀ Wildlife watchers help common toads cross the road to reach their breeding ponds in safety.

▲ When it is time to hibernate, a frog must find a safe, damp place to stay.

215 When the weather turns especially cold, amphibians often hide away. They simply hibernate in the mud at the bottom of ponds or under stones and logs. This means that they go to sleep in the autumn and don't wake up until spring.

Gills

▶ This is a mudpuppy – a type of salamander. It spends its whole life underwater and breathes using its frilly gills.

▲ Pygmy marbled newts avoid getting too hot by hiding under rotting wood or by resting in mud during the day.

216 Journeys to breeding grounds may be up to 5 kilometres – a long way for an animal only a few centimetres in length. This is like a person walking 90 kilometres away without a map! The animals find their way by scent, landmarks, the Earth's magnetic field and the Sun's position.

Water babies

217 Amphibians live in water and on land. Most are born and grow up in fresh water such as ponds, pools, streams and rivers. They move onto dry land when they are adults and return to water to breed.

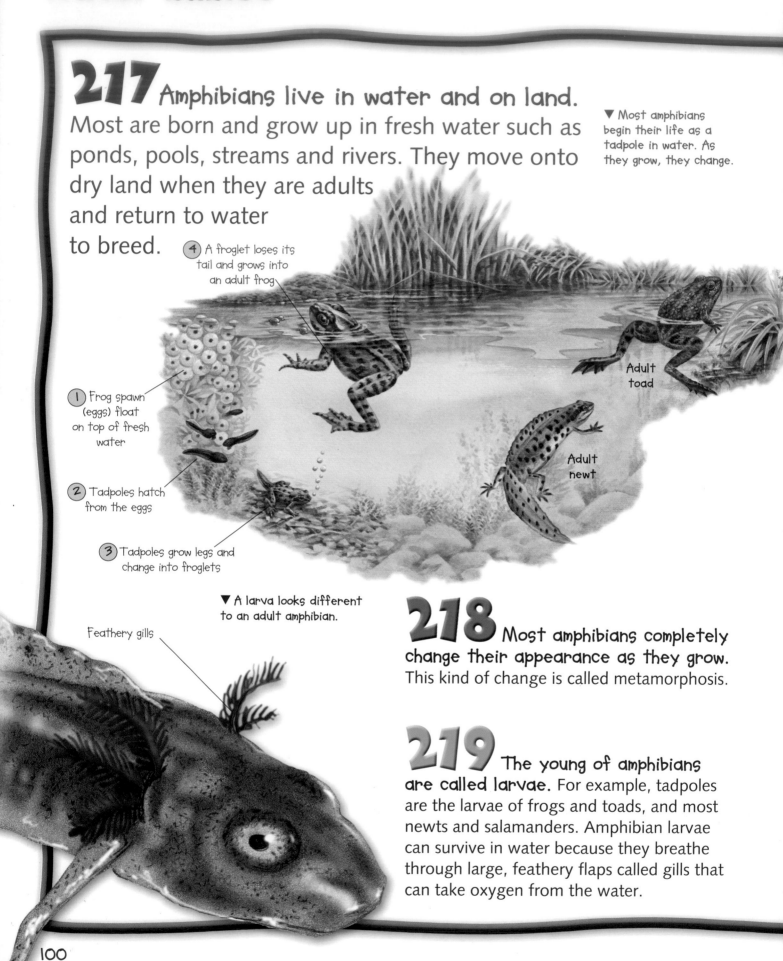

▼ Most amphibians begin their life as a tadpole in water. As they grow, they change.

④ A froglet loses its tail and grows into an adult frog

① Frog spawn (eggs) float on top of fresh water

② Tadpoles hatch from the eggs

③ Tadpoles grow legs and change into froglets

Adult toad

Adult newt

▼ A larva looks different to an adult amphibian.

Feathery gills

218 Most amphibians completely change their appearance as they grow. This kind of change is called metamorphosis.

219 The young of amphibians are called larvae. For example, tadpoles are the larvae of frogs and toads, and most newts and salamanders. Amphibian larvae can survive in water because they breathe through large, feathery flaps called gills that can take oxygen from the water.

▲ An axolotl is a strange creature that remains a tadpole all its life.

220
The axolotl is an amphibian that has never grown up. This type of water-living salamander has never developed beyond the larval stage. It does, however, develop far enough to be able to breed.

I DON'T BELIEVE IT!

The male South American Surinam toad is quite an acrobat. When mating underwater, it has to press the eggs onto its mate's back. The eggs remain there until they hatch.

▼ Toads can lay hundreds — even thousands — of eggs at a time.

221
The majority of amphibians lay soft eggs. These may be in a jelly-like string or clump of tiny eggs called spawn, as with frogs and toads. Newts lay their eggs singly.

222
A few amphibians give birth to live young instead of laying eggs. The eggs of the fire salamander, for example, stay inside their mother, where the young hatch out and develop. The female then gives birth to young that are like miniature adults.

Land babies

223 The majority of reptiles spend their whole lives away from water. They are very well adapted for life on dry land. Some do spend time in the water, but most reptiles lay their eggs on land.

► A leatherback turtle uses her hind legs to dig a burrow in the sand, and then lays her clutch of round eggs inside.

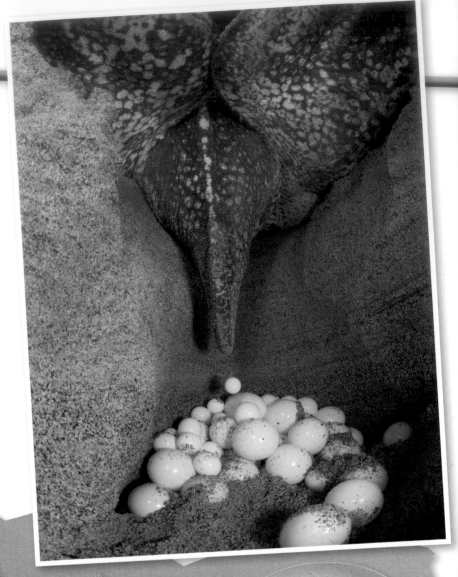

Alligator

Ground python

Javan bloodsucker lizard

Galapagos giant tortoise

▲ Reptiles lay eggs of different shapes and sizes.

224 Most reptile eggs are much tougher than those of amphibians. This is because they must survive life out of the water. Lizards and snakes lay eggs with leathery shells. Crocodile and tortoise eggs have a hard shell rather like birds' eggs.

225 The eggs feed and protect the young developing inside them. Yolk provides food for the developing young, which is called an embryo. The shell protects the embryo from the outside world, but also allows vital oxygen into the egg.

① When fully developed, a baby snake uses the egg tooth on the tip of its snout to tear a hole in the egg.

② The snake tastes the air with its forked tongue. It may stay in the shell for a few days.

③ Eventually, the snake uncoils its body and wriggles free of the egg.

④ The baby snake slides along in S-shaped curves to begin its life in the wild.

AMAZING EGGS

Reptile eggs are like birds' eggs. Next time you eat an egg, rinse out half an empty eggshell, fill it with water and wait a while. See how no water escapes! Wash your hands well once you're done. Like this bird's eggshell, reptile eggshells stop the egg from drying out, although they let air in and are tough enough to protect the embryo.

226 Young reptiles hatch out of eggs as miniature adults. They do not undergo a change, or metamorphosis, like amphibians do.

▶ A slow worm protects her eggs inside her body, until they are ready to hatch.

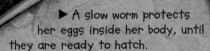

227 Some snakes and lizards, like slow worms, don't lay eggs. Instead, they give birth to fully developed live young. Animals that do this are called 'viviparous'.

Little and large

228 Reptiles and amphibians come in every shape and size. There are more than 9000 species (types) of reptiles and 7000 species of amphibians. They range from tiny frogs to giant, dinosaur-like lizards.

229 The largest reptile award goes to the saltwater crocodile from around the Indian and west Pacific Oceans. It can grow to a staggering 7 metres from nose to tail – an average adult human is not even 2 metres tall! Japan's cold streams are home to the largest amphibian – a giant salamander that is around 1.5 metres and weighs up to 40 kilograms.

▲ Chinese salamanders are often heavier than their Japanese cousins. They can weigh up to 65 kg – more than a child!

▼ Most saltwater crocodiles grow to be about 5 metres in length. These massive predators are called 'salties' in Australia.

230 The world's tiniest reptiles are dwarf geckos. The smallest one discovered so far measured just 16 millimetres in length. A Brazilian frog is one of the smallest amphibians. Its body length is just 9.8 millimetres – that makes it small enough to sit on your thumbnail!

▶ A European tree frog is up to 50 millimetres long.

▼ A female pygmy leaf chameleon is just 34 millimetres long, but the male is even smaller!

ACTUAL SIZE

Adaptable animals

231 Many reptiles and amphibians have special adaptations to help them live safely and easily in their surroundings. For example, crocodiles have a special flap in their throats that means that they can open their mouth underwater without breathing in water.

232 Geckos can climb up vertical surfaces or even upside down. They are able to cling on because they have five wide-spreading toes, each with sticky toe-pads, on each foot. These strong pads are covered with millions of tiny hairs that grip surfaces tightly.

◄ Tokay geckos are one of the largest geckos. They can reach up to 35 centimetres in length and are usually brightly patterned.

233 Tortoises and turtles have hard, bony shells for protection. They form a suit of armour that protects them from predators (animals that might hunt and eat them) and also from the hot Sun.

LEARNING MORE

Pick a favourite reptile or amphibian and then find out as much as you can about it. List all the ways you think it is especially well adapted to deal with its lifestyle and habitat.

► Colourful chameleons often have a row of spines on their backs to make them look fierce.

234 Chameleons have adapted well to their way of life in the trees. They have long toes that can grip branches firmly, and a long tail that grips like another hand. Tails that can grip like this are called 'prehensile'. Chameleons are also known for being able to change their colour to blend in with their surroundings. This is called 'camouflage', and is something that many other reptiles and amphibians use.

235 The flattened tails of newts make them expert swimmers. Newts are salamanders that spend most of their lives in water, so they need to be able to get about speedily in this environment.

▼ Newts swim quickly to chase prey such as shrimps and tadpoles.

236 Some amphibians use gills to breathe underwater. Blood flows inside the feathery gills, at the same time as water flows over the outside. As the water flows past the gills, oxygen passes out of the water, straight into the blood.

Natural show-offs

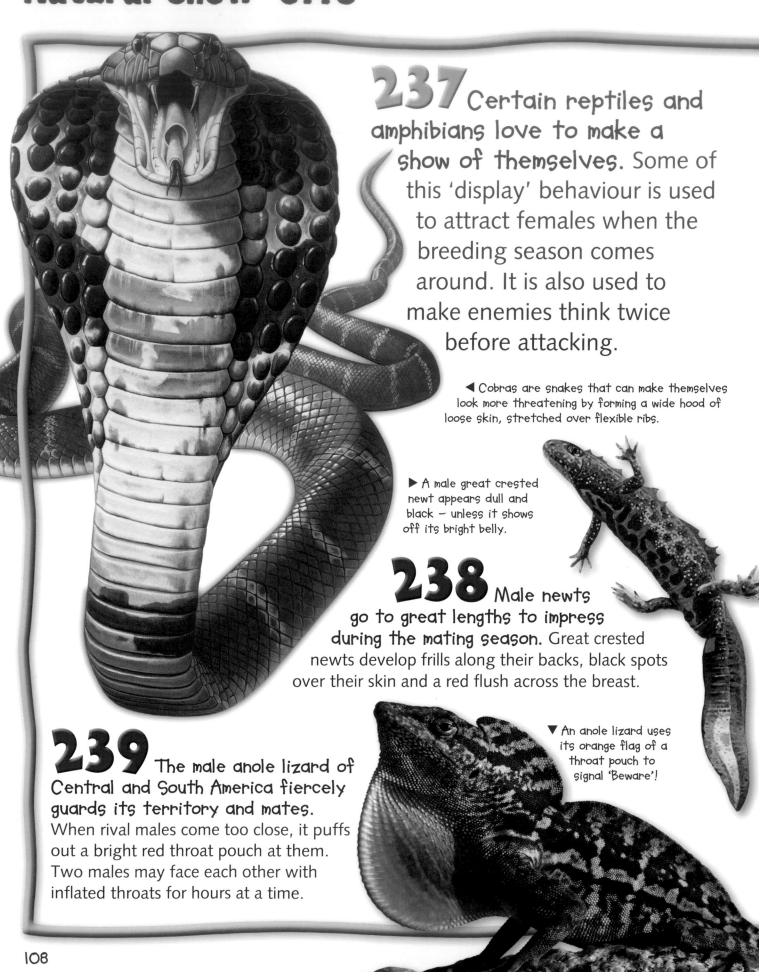

237 Certain reptiles and amphibians love to make a show of themselves. Some of this 'display' behaviour is used to attract females when the breeding season comes around. It is also used to make enemies think twice before attacking.

◀ Cobras are snakes that can make themselves look more threatening by forming a wide hood of loose skin, stretched over flexible ribs.

▶ A male great crested newt appears dull and black – unless it shows off its bright belly.

238 Male newts go to great lengths to impress during the mating season. Great crested newts develop frills along their backs, black spots over their skin and a red flush across the breast.

239 The male anole lizard of Central and South America fiercely guards its territory and mates. When rival males come too close, it puffs out a bright red throat pouch at them. Two males may face each other with inflated throats for hours at a time.

▼ An anole lizard uses its orange flag of a throat pouch to signal 'Beware'!

240 Many frogs and toads puff themselves up. Toads can inflate their bodies to appear more frightening. Frogs and toads can also puff out their throat pouches. This makes their croaking love-calls to mates and 'back off' calls to enemies much louder.

▲ A green tree frog uses its air-filled throat pouch to impress a female.

241 A frilled lizard in full display is an amazing sight. This lizard has a large flap of neck skin that normally lies flat. When faced by a predator, it spreads this out to form a huge, stiff ruff that makes the lizard look bigger and scarier!

242 Male monitor lizards have wrestling competitions! At the beginning of the mating season they compete to try to win the females. They rear up on their hind legs and wrestle until the weaker one gives up.

▲ A frilled lizard scares predators away with its huge frill, large yellow mouth and a loud hiss.

Sensitive creatures

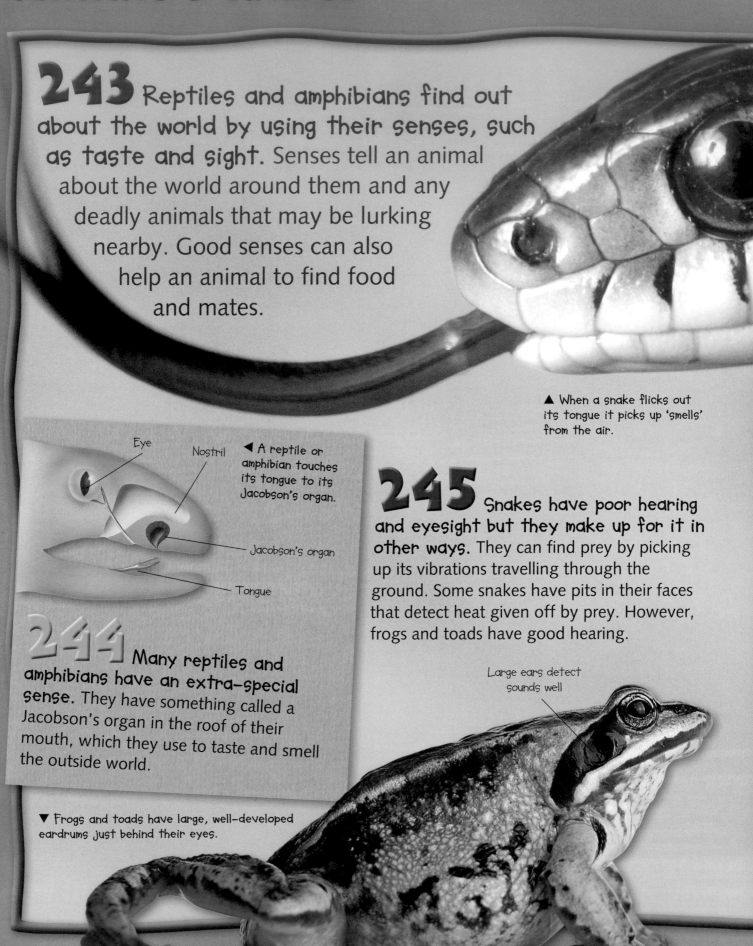

243 Reptiles and amphibians find out about the world by using their senses, such as taste and sight. Senses tell an animal about the world around them and any deadly animals that may be lurking nearby. Good senses can also help an animal to find food and mates.

▲ When a snake flicks out its tongue it picks up 'smells' from the air.

Eye

Nostril

◀ A reptile or amphibian touches its tongue to its Jacobson's organ.

Jacobson's organ

Tongue

244 Many reptiles and amphibians have an extra-special sense. They have something called a Jacobson's organ in the roof of their mouth, which they use to taste and smell the outside world.

245 Snakes have poor hearing and eyesight but they make up for it in other ways. They can find prey by picking up its vibrations travelling through the ground. Some snakes have pits in their faces that detect heat given off by prey. However, frogs and toads have good hearing.

Large ears detect sounds well

▼ Frogs and toads have large, well-developed eardrums just behind their eyes.

246 Geckos and iguanas have large eyes and good eyesight. They are a type of lizard that can't blink. Instead of having movable eyelids like humans, they have fixed, transparent 'spectacles' over their eyes. Most lizards have good sight – they need it to hunt down their small, fast insect prey.

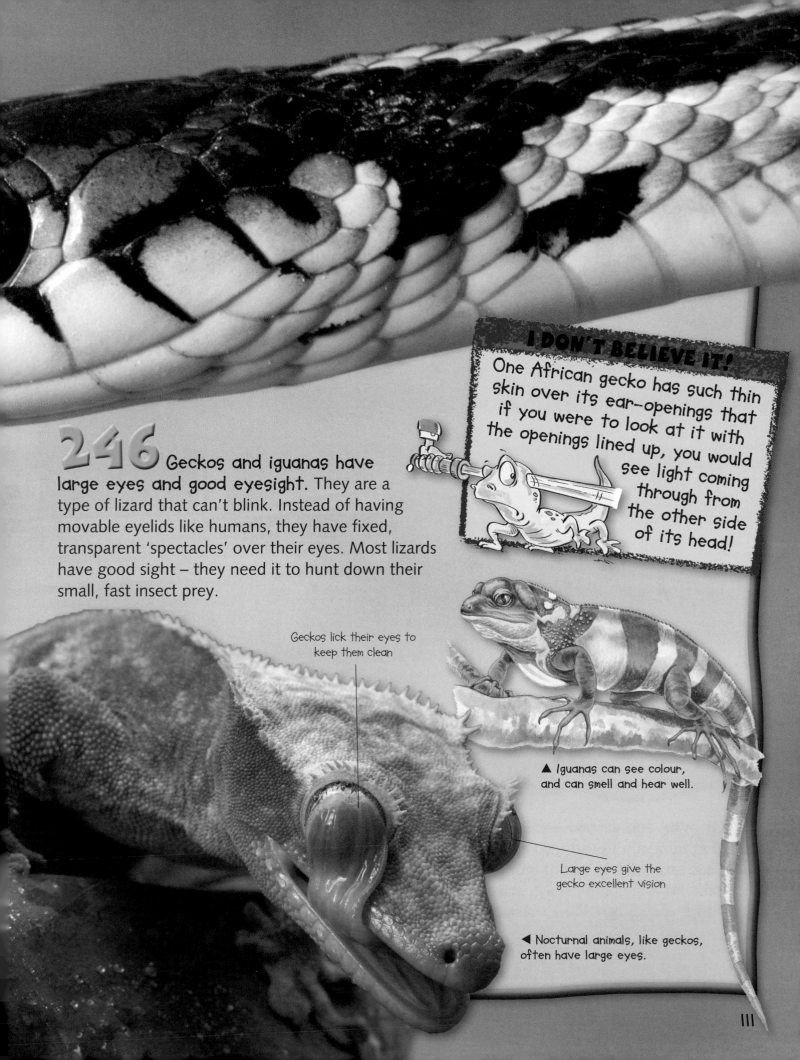

I DON'T BELIEVE IT!

One African gecko has such thin skin over its ear-openings that if you were to look at it with the openings lined up, you would see light coming through from the other side of its head!

Geckos lick their eyes to keep them clean

▲ Iguanas can see colour, and can smell and hear well.

Large eyes give the gecko excellent vision

◄ Nocturnal animals, like geckos, often have large eyes.

Feeling hungry

Oesophagus

Liver and
gall bladder

▼ This Northern leopard frog is eating a
dragonfly. Food passes along the digestive
system, where chemicals (called enzymes) break
it up into smaller pieces to release energy.

Stomach

Kidney

Large
intestine

Dragonfly prey

Mouth

Small
intestine

247 All amphibians and most reptiles are meat-eaters. They don't have teeth, so many of them eat bugs that they can swallow whole. Once food goes down the animal's throat it must be digested.

◄ A chameleon's
tongue can be as
long as its body.

248 The chameleon lizard is a highly efficient hunting machine. Both eyes move separately from each other, so the chameleon can look in two directions at once. When a tasty fly buzzes past, the chameleon shoots out an incredibly long tongue in a fraction of a second and draws the fly back into its mouth.

249

Salamanders creep up slowly before striking. They move gradually towards prey and then suddenly seize it with their tongue, or between their sharp teeth.

250

Large reptiles can manage massive meals! Crocodiles and big snakes open their jaws wide enough to bite animals that are as big as themselves. Crocodiles must bite lumps of meat off their prey to swallow, and they also swallow stones to help grind the food up.

◀ Crocodiles wait in shallow water for animals to come and drink, then leap up and drag their prey under the water.

BE A CHAMELEON

Like a chameleon, you need two eyes to judge distances easily. Close one eye, hold a finger out in front of you, and then try to touch this fingertip with the other. Now open both eyes and you'll find it a lot easier. Two eyes give your brain two slightly different angles to look at the object, so it is easier to tell how far away it is.

Fliers and leapers

251 Some reptiles and amphibians can take to the air – if only for a few seconds. This helps animals to travel further, escape predators or swoop down on passing prey before it gets away.

▼ A Blandford's flying lizard has thin wing-like flaps of skin that are supported by 5–7 pairs of ribs. It can travel up to 10 metres between trees.

253 Even certain kinds of snake can glide. The flying snake lives in the tropical forests of southern Asia. It can jump between branches or glide through the air in 'S' movements.

252 Reptiles that glide turn their bodies into parachutes. They are able to spread their bodies out, making them wide so they catch the air and slow the animal's descent.

254 Flying geckos have wide, webbed feet. They use flaps of skin along their sides to help control their flight as they leap between trees. Flying geckos take to the air to avoid danger.

▼ The four webbed feet of a Wallace's flying frog help it to glide.

255 Some frogs can glide. Deep in the steamy rainforests of Southeast Asia and South America, tree frogs flit from tree to tree. Some can glide as far as 12 metres, clinging to their landing spot with suckers on their feet.

256 Frogs and toads use their powerful hind legs for hopping or jumping. The greatest frog leaper comes from Africa. Known as the rocket frog, it has been known to jump up to 4.2 metres.

① The powerful muscles in the frog's hind legs push off

② In mid-leap, the frog's hind legs are fully stretched out, its front legs are held back and its eyes are closed for protection

③ As it lands, its body arches and the front legs act as a brake

QUIZ

1. Where does the flying snake live?

2. How far can some tree frogs glide?

3. Which frog has been known to jump up to 4.2 metres?

Answers:
1. In the tropical forests of southern Asia 2. 12 metres 3.The rocket frog

Slitherers and crawlers

257 Most reptiles, and some amphibians, spend much of their time creeping, crawling and slithering along the ground. Scientists call the study of reptiles and amphibians 'herpetology', which comes from a Greek word meaning 'to creep or crawl'.

SLITHER AND SLIDE

Make your own slithery snake! First, collect as many cotton reels as you can, then paint them lots of bright colours. Next, cut a forked tongue and some snake eyes out of some paper. Stick them onto one of the reels to make a head. Now thread your reels onto a piece of string. Make sure the head isn't in the middle!

258 A snake's skin does not grow with its body. This means that it has to shed its skin to grow bigger. When a snake sheds its skin it is said to be moulting. Snakes moult at least once a year.

▲ Sidewinders have an unusual movement that allows them to slither over hot sand at speed.

▲ A moult begins at a snake's nose and can take up to 14 days to complete.

259 Some frogs and toads also shed their skin. The European toad sheds its skin several times during the summer – and then eats it! This recycles the goodness in the toad's skin.

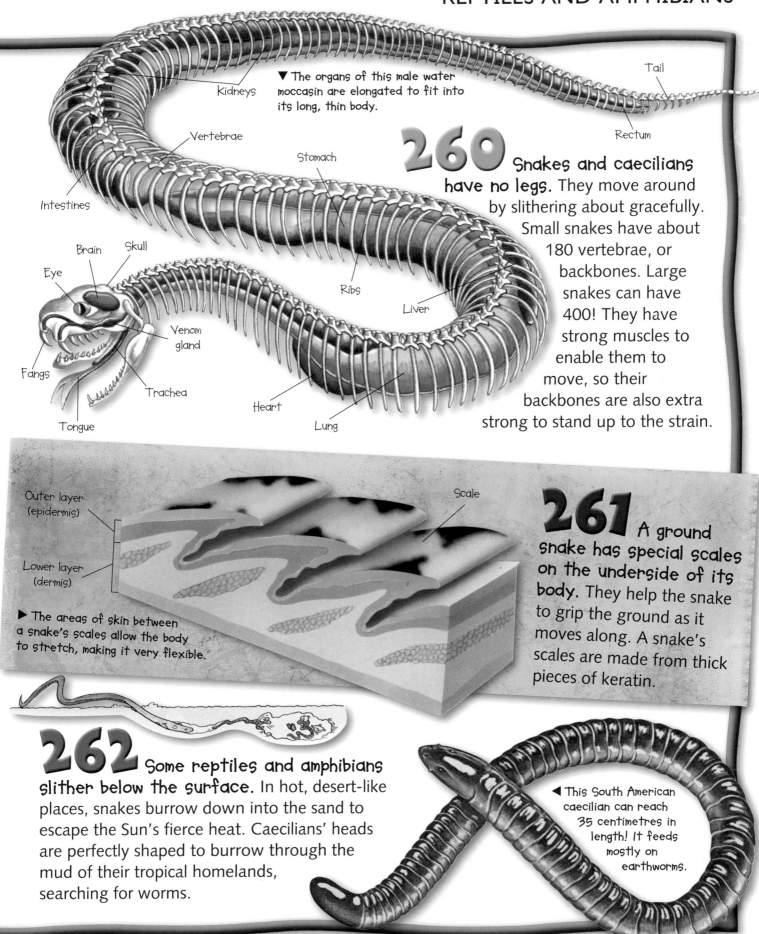

▼ The organs of this male water moccasin are elongated to fit into its long, thin body.

Kidneys

Vertebrae

Stomach

Tail

Rectum

Intestines

Brain

Skull

Eye

Venom gland

Fangs

Trachea

Tongue

Heart

Ribs

Liver

Lung

260
Snakes and caecilians have no legs. They move around by slithering about gracefully. Small snakes have about 180 vertebrae, or backbones. Large snakes can have 400! They have strong muscles to enable them to move, so their backbones are also extra strong to stand up to the strain.

Outer layer (epidermis)

Scale

Lower layer (dermis)

▶ The areas of skin between a snake's scales allow the body to stretch, making it very flexible.

261
A ground snake has special scales on the underside of its body. They help the snake to grip the ground as it moves along. A snake's scales are made from thick pieces of keratin.

262
Some reptiles and amphibians slither below the surface. In hot, desert-like places, snakes burrow down into the sand to escape the Sun's fierce heat. Caecilians' heads are perfectly shaped to burrow through the mud of their tropical homelands, searching for worms.

◀ This South American caecilian can reach 35 centimetres in length! It feeds mostly on earthworms.

117

Fast and slow

263 The reptile and amphibian worlds contain their fair share of fast and slow movers. However, a predator may be able to seize the slow-moving tortoise, but it will struggle to bite through its armour-plated shell!

264 Tortoises are among the slowest animals on Earth. The top speed for a giant tortoise is 5 metres a minute! These giant reptiles live on the small Galapagos islands in the Pacific Ocean and the Seychelles.

265 Some lizards can run on water. Basilisks from Costa Rica and Philippine sail-fin water dragons leap into the water to escape from predators. They are good swimmers, but their most impressive trick is to sprint across the water's surface on their long hind legs.

◄ The enormous Galapagos giant tortoise may weigh as much as four adult humans.

FLAT RACE

Get a group of friends together and hold your own animal race day! Each of you cuts a flat animal shape – a frog or tortoise for example – out of paper or light card. Add details with coloured pencils or pens. Now race your animals along the ground to the finishing line by flapping a newspaper or a magazine behind them.

▼ A plumed basilisk uses its tail and wide feet to stay on the water's surface as it runs.

266 One of the world's slowest animals is the lizard-like tuatara. When resting, it breathes just once an hour, and may still be growing when it is 35 years old! Their slow lifestyle in part means that tuataras can live to be 120 years old!

▲ Tuataras live on a few small islands off the coast of New Zealand.

267 The fastest reptile in the world is the speedy spiny-tailed iguana. It can reach top speeds of 34.9 kilometres an hour. Racerunner lizards come a close second – in 1941 one of these racing reptiles ran at 29 kilometres an hour.

268 The fastest snake on land is the deadly black mamba. These shy African snakes are nervous reptiles that are easily scared – and quick to attack. This combination makes a mamba a snake to avoid!

Champion swimmers

269 Amphibians are well known for their links with water, but some types of reptile are also aquatic (live in the water). Different types of amphibian and reptile have developed all kinds of ways of tackling watery lifestyles.

▼ Marine iguanas dive into chilly seawater to graze on seaweed. They can dive up to 9 metres at a time, but then have to bask to warm up again.

I DON'T BELIEVE IT!

Floating sea snakes can be surrounded by fish who gather at the snake's tail to avoid being eaten. When the snake fancies a snack, it swims backwards, fooling the fish into thinking its head is its tail!

270 Newts and salamanders swim rather like fish. They make an 'S' shape as they move. Many have flat tails that help to propel them through the water.

Eastern newt

▲▼ Newts are good swimmers and spend most of their lives in water.

Rough-skinned newt

271 Toads and frogs propel themselves by kicking back with their hind legs. They use their front legs as a brake for landing when they dive into the water. Large, webbed feet act like flippers, helping them to push through the water.

① Frog draws its legs up

③ The main kick back with toes spread propels the frog forward through the water

② Then pushes its feet out to the side

④ Frog closes its toes and draws its legs in and up for the next kick

272 A swimming snake may seem unlikely, but most snakes are experts in the water. Sea snakes can stay submerged for five hours and move rapidly through the water. European grass snakes are also good swimmers. They have to be because they eat animals that live around water.

▼ Sea snakes return to land to lay eggs.

Yellow-bellied sea snake

▼ Green turtles took to the sea about 150 million years ago.

273 Sea turtles have light, flat shells so they can move along more easily under water. Some have managed speeds of 29 kilometres an hour. Their flipper-like front legs 'fly' through the water. Their back legs form mini-rudders for steering.

Banded sea snake

Nature's tanks

274 Tortoises and turtles are like armoured tanks – slow but well-protected by their shells. Tortoises live on land and eat mainly plants. Some turtles are flesh-eaters that live in the salty sea. Other turtles, some of which are called terrapins, live in freshwater lakes and rivers.

I DON'T BELIEVE IT!

A giant tortoise can support a one tonne weight. This means that it could be used as a jack to lift up a car – but far kinder and easier simply to go to a local garage!

◀ An eagle's huge talons grip onto a tortoise. The bird will fly with the tortoise, then drop it from a height to break its tough shell.

275 When danger threatens, tortoises can quickly retreat into their mobile homes. They simply draw their head, tail and legs into their shell.

▶ A tortoise's shell is part of its body. It cannot climb out of its shell, which is attached to its skeleton.

276 Tortoises and turtles are ancient members of the reptile world. They are the oldest living reptiles, and might have been around with the very first dinosaurs, about 200 million years ago. They also live longer than almost any other animal – some for up to 150 years!

Indian softshell turtle

Leopard tortoise

Matamata turtle

Hawksbill turtle

▲ Tortoises and turtles belong to a group of reptiles called Chelonians. They all have four limbs, a hard shell and a horny beak for a mouth. Their shells can be leathery or covered in plates.

277 Some sea turtles are among nature's greatest travellers. The green turtle migrates an amazing 2000 kilometres from its feeding grounds off the coast of Brazil to breeding sites such as Ascension Island, in the South Atlantic.

Dangerous enemies

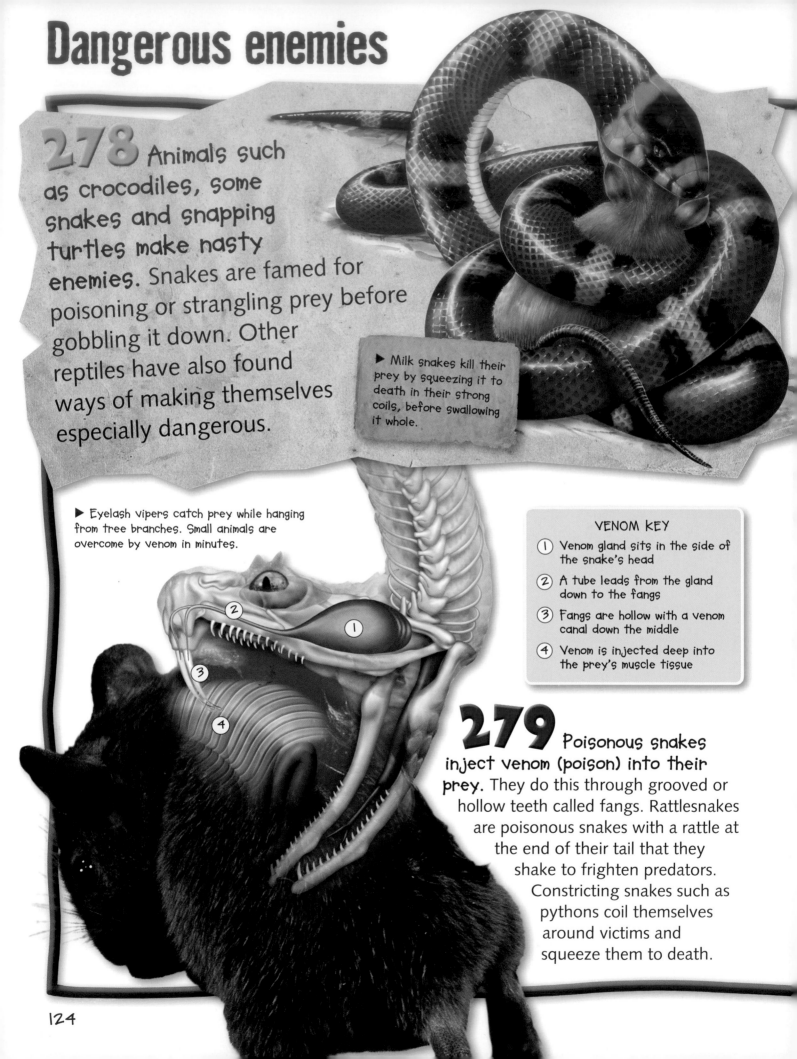

278 Animals such as crocodiles, some snakes and snapping turtles make nasty enemies. Snakes are famed for poisoning or strangling prey before gobbling it down. Other reptiles have also found ways of making themselves especially dangerous.

▶ Milk snakes kill their prey by squeezing it to death in their strong coils, before swallowing it whole.

▶ Eyelash vipers catch prey while hanging from tree branches. Small animals are overcome by venom in minutes.

VENOM KEY
① Venom gland sits in the side of the snake's head
② A tube leads from the gland down to the fangs
③ Fangs are hollow with a venom canal down the middle
④ Venom is injected deep into the prey's muscle tissue

279 Poisonous snakes inject venom (poison) into their prey. They do this through grooved or hollow teeth called fangs. Rattlesnakes are poisonous snakes with a rattle at the end of their tail that they shake to frighten predators. Constricting snakes such as pythons coil themselves around victims and squeeze them to death.

QUIZ

1. How does an alligator snapping turtle lure its prey?
2. How do poisonous snakes inject venom (poison) into their prey?
3. Which amphibian has bright yellow spots or stripes?

Answers:
1. By waving the tip of its tongue, which looks like a juicy worm 2. Through grooved or hollow teeth called fangs 3. A fire salamander

▼ Alligator snapping turtles can deliver one of the strongest bites in the animal world.

280 The alligator snapping turtle looks like a rough rock as it lies on the ocean floor. This cunning turtle has an extra trick up its sleeve. The tip of its tongue looks like a juicy worm, which it waves at passing prey to lure them into its jaws.

BEWARE! POISONOUS

▶ A fire salamander sprays foul poisons at a predator.

◀ The skin of a strawberry poison-dart frog is coated with deadly poison.

281 Bright patterns on some amphibians' skin warn predators. Their skin may be foul-tasting or cause irritation. Arrow-poison frogs from South America's rainforests have very bright colours, while fire salamanders have bright yellow spots or stripes.

125

Clever mimics

282 Reptiles and amphibians are masters of disguise. Some blend into their surroundings naturally, while others can change their appearance – perfect for avoiding predators or sneaking up on prey.

283 Frogs and toads are experts in the art of camouflage (blending with surroundings). Many are coloured shades of green or green-brown, to look just like leaves, grass or tree bark.

▶ A mossy frog's coloured and bumpy skin helps it blend into a tree trunk's mottled surface.

ANIMAL DISGUISE

Make a mask of your favourite reptile or amphibian from a round piece of card or a paper plate. Look at the pictures in this book to help you add details and colour it in. Carefully cut some eye holes, and then attach some string or elastic to the sides to hold it to your head.

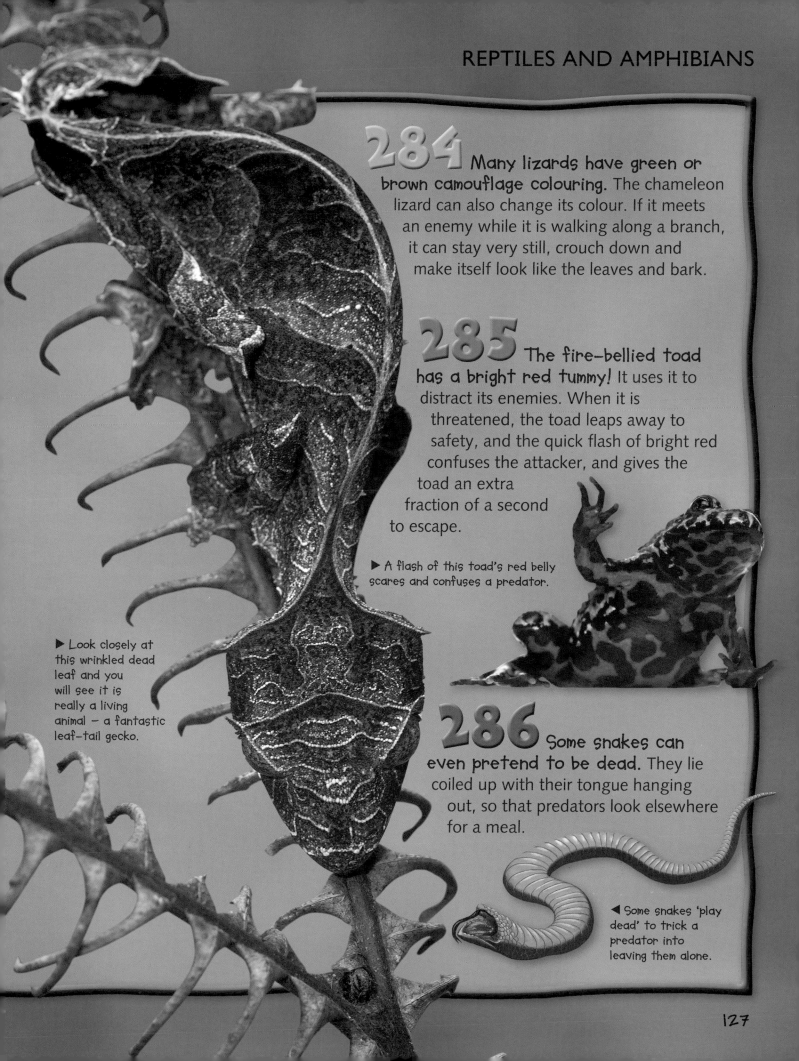

284 Many lizards have green or brown camouflage colouring. The chameleon lizard can also change its colour. If it meets an enemy while it is walking along a branch, it can stay very still, crouch down and make itself look like the leaves and bark.

285 The fire-bellied toad has a bright red tummy! It uses it to distract its enemies. When it is threatened, the toad leaps away to safety, and the quick flash of bright red confuses the attacker, and gives the toad an extra fraction of a second to escape.

▶ A flash of this toad's red belly scares and confuses a predator.

▶ Look closely at this wrinkled dead leaf and you will see it is really a living animal – a fantastic leaf-tail gecko.

286 Some snakes can even pretend to be dead. They lie coiled up with their tongue hanging out, so that predators look elsewhere for a meal.

◀ Some snakes 'play dead' to trick a predator into leaving them alone.

Escape artists

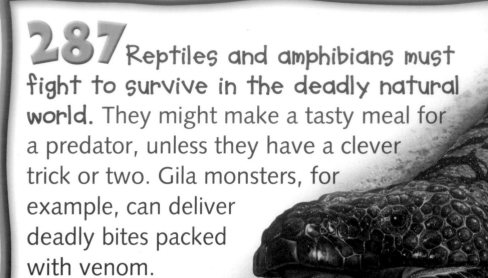

287 Reptiles and amphibians must fight to survive in the deadly natural world. They might make a tasty meal for a predator, unless they have a clever trick or two. Gila monsters, for example, can deliver deadly bites packed with venom.

▶ A gila monster must bite and chew to release its venom.

288 Some salamanders and lizards have detachable tails. If a predator grabs a five-lined tree skink lizard by the tail, it will be left holding a twitching blue tail! The tail does grow back.

289 Spraying an attacker with blood is a good trick. Desert horned lizards puff themselves up, hiss and squirt blood out of their eyes when they are scared.

◀ A desert horned lizard's bloody face is fearsome.

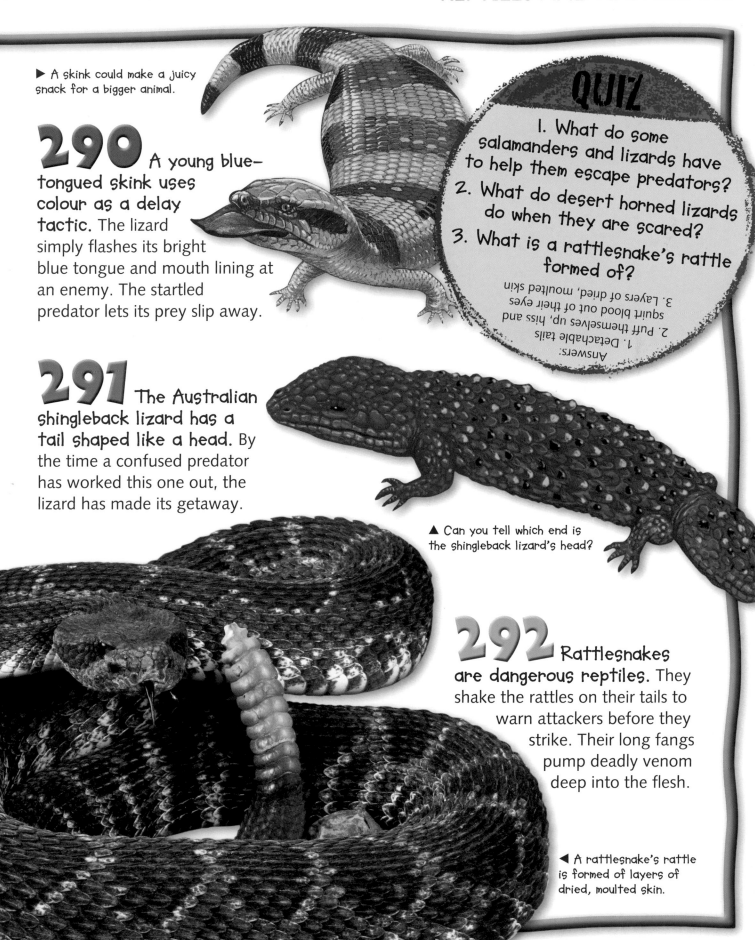

▶ A skink could make a juicy snack for a bigger animal.

290 A young blue-tongued skink uses colour as a delay tactic. The lizard simply flashes its bright blue tongue and mouth lining at an enemy. The startled predator lets its prey slip away.

291 The Australian shingleback lizard has a tail shaped like a head. By the time a confused predator has worked this one out, the lizard has made its getaway.

▲ Can you tell which end is the shingleback lizard's head?

292 Rattlesnakes are dangerous reptiles. They shake the rattles on their tails to warn attackers before they strike. Their long fangs pump deadly venom deep into the flesh.

◀ A rattlesnake's rattle is formed of layers of dried, moulted skin.

Mega reptiles

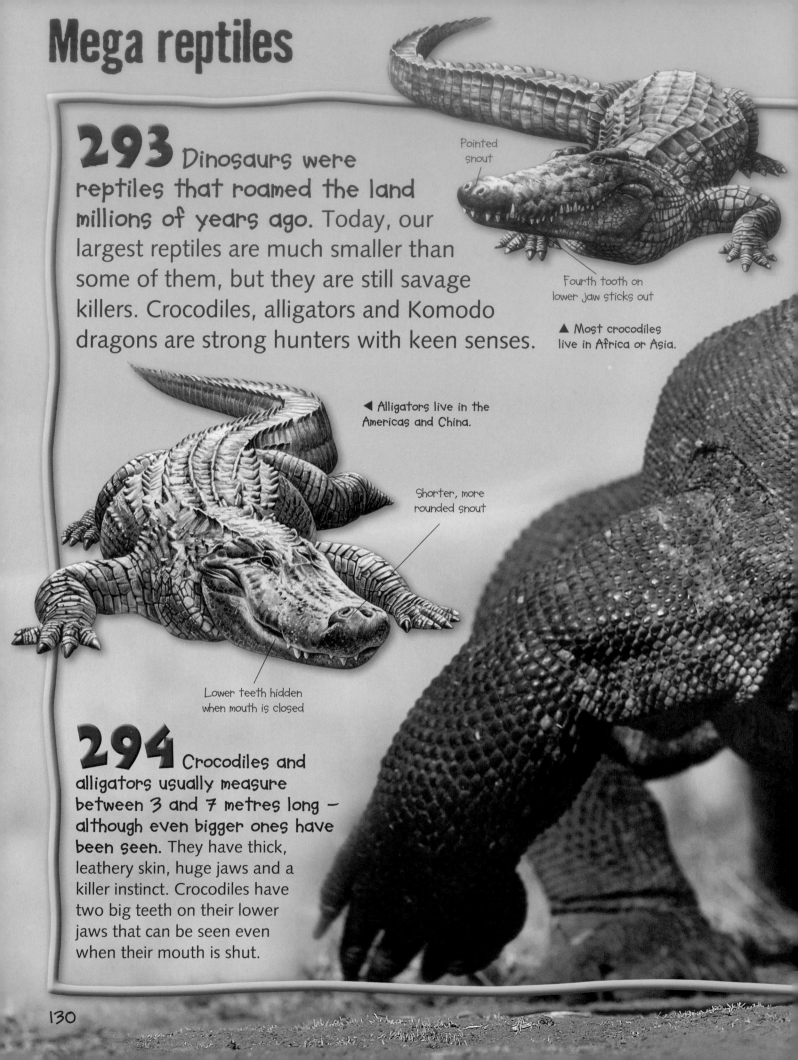

293 Dinosaurs were reptiles that roamed the land millions of years ago. Today, our largest reptiles are much smaller than some of them, but they are still savage killers. Crocodiles, alligators and Komodo dragons are strong hunters with keen senses.

Pointed snout

Fourth tooth on lower jaw sticks out

▲ Most crocodiles live in Africa or Asia.

◄ Alligators live in the Americas and China.

Shorter, more rounded snout

Lower teeth hidden when mouth is closed

294 Crocodiles and alligators usually measure between 3 and 7 metres long — although even bigger ones have been seen. They have thick, leathery skin, huge jaws and a killer instinct. Crocodiles have two big teeth on their lower jaws that can be seen even when their mouth is shut.

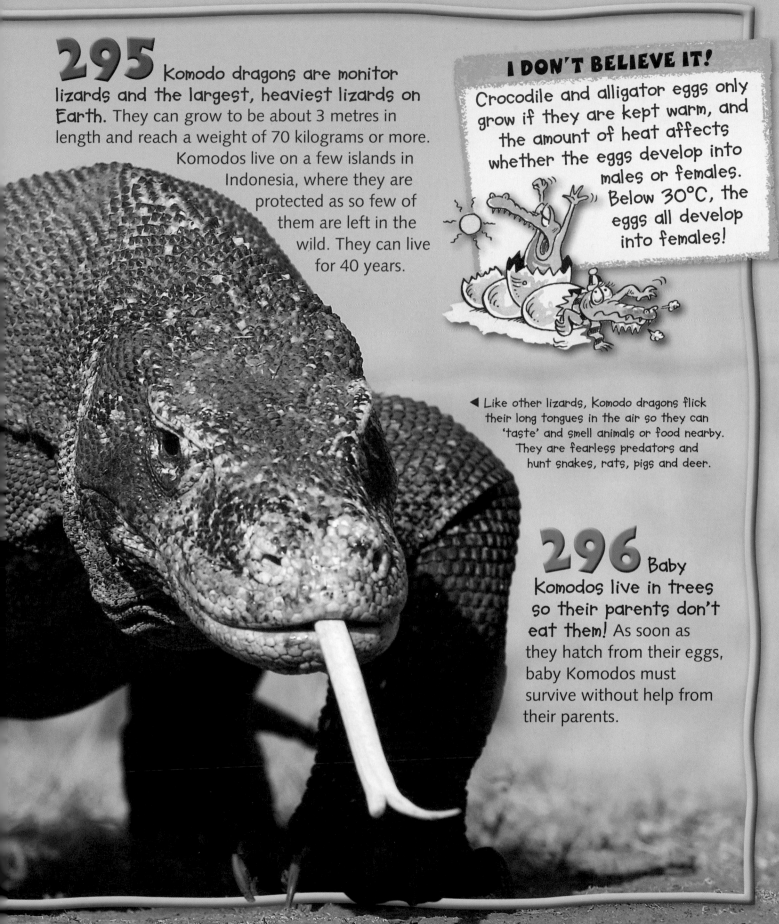

295 Komodo dragons are monitor lizards and the largest, heaviest lizards on Earth. They can grow to be about 3 metres in length and reach a weight of 70 kilograms or more. Komodos live on a few islands in Indonesia, where they are protected as so few of them are left in the wild. They can live for 40 years.

I DON'T BELIEVE IT!

Crocodile and alligator eggs only grow if they are kept warm, and the amount of heat affects whether the eggs develop into males or females. Below 30°C, the eggs all develop into females!

◀ Like other lizards, Komodo dragons flick their long tongues in the air so they can 'taste' and smell animals or food nearby. They are fearless predators and hunt snakes, rats, pigs and deer.

296 Baby Komodos live in trees so their parents don't eat them! As soon as they hatch from their eggs, baby Komodos must survive without help from their parents.

In danger

297 One-third of all reptiles and amphibians are at risk of dying out forever. They are at risk of extinction because they are losing their habitats (homes) or because they have been hunted.

298 Green turtles may die out because people steal their eggs to sell as food. Their breeding beaches have also been taken over by hotels or houses, or ruined with pollution. Adult green turtles are captured in the seas around Asia and then eaten.

► Scientists hope to save green turtles from extinction. They tag them and follow their movements across the oceans.

Geochelone abingdoni
R.I.P.
24 de Junio, 2012 (June 24th, 2012)

Solitario George | Lonesome George

Prometemos contar tu historia | We promise to tell your story
y transmitir tu mensaje de conservación | and to share your conservation message

▲ Lonesome George's death has inspired many people to save the last giant tortoises.

299 Lonesome George was a type of giant tortoise and the last of his kind. He lived on the Galapagos Islands, where turtles were once common reptiles. When he died in 2012, George's sub-species became extinct forever.

300 Amphibians are at risk from climate change. They need their homes to stay warm and damp, but pollution is changing our planet's weather systems. Many frogs and toads have also died from a skin disease that has spread around the world.

▲ Panamanian golden frogs are probably extinct in the wild.

QUIZ

1. In what year did Lonesome George die?

2. How are scientists trying to save green turtles from extinction?

3. Which frogs are probably extinct in the wild?

Answers:
1. 2012 2. By tagging them and following their movements across the oceans 3. Panamanian golden frogs

BIRDS

301 A bird has two legs, a pair of wings and a body that is covered with feathers. Birds are one of the types of animals we see most often in the wild. They live all over the world – everywhere from Antarctica to the hottest deserts. They range in size from the huge ostrich, which can be up to 2.75 metres tall, to the tiny bee hummingbird, which is scarcely bigger than a real bee.

▲ Baya weaver birds are found across South and Southeast Asia. As their name suggests, weaver birds build nests by weaving together strips of plant material and leaves.

The bird world

302 There are over 9000 different types, or species, of bird. These have been organized by scientists into 29 groups called orders, which contain many different species. The largest is the Passeriformes order.

▼ This chaffinch is in the Passeriformes order. More than half of all bird species belong to this order.

Wings

Crown

Bill, or beak

Throat

Breast

Passeriformes order: Includes robins, sparrows and wrens

Toes

Two legs

Tail

Common swift

Apodiformes order: Swifts and hummingbirds

Keel-billed toucan

Piciformes order: Toucans and woodpeckers

Blue-and-yellow macaw

Psitticiformes order: Parrots, cockatoos and lorikeets

Pied avocet

Charadiiformes order: Waders, gulls and auks

▲ The shape of a bird's beak can be used to decide which order a bird belongs to. These pictures show examples from the largest orders.

303 All birds have wings. These are the bird's front limbs. There are many different wing shapes. Birds that soar in the sky for hours, such as eagles, have long, broad wings. These help them use air currents. Small, fast-flying birds such as swifts have slim, pointed wings.

▶ Feathers have different shapes, sizes and textures, suited to the jobs they do.

Tail feather

Flight feather

Contour (body) feather

Down feather

304 Birds are the only creatures that have feathers. They are made of keratin – the same material as our hair and nails. Feathers keep a bird warm, and its wing and tail feathers help it to fly. Some birds have colourful feathers to help attract mates or blend in with their surroundings – camouflage.

305
All birds have a beak, or bill, for eating. The beak is made of bone and is covered with a hard material called horn. Birds have different kinds of beak for different types of food. Insect-eating birds tend to have thin, sharp beaks for picking up their tiny prey. The parrot's strong beak is ideal for cracking nuts. Hunting birds, such as goshawks, have powerful hooked beaks for tearing flesh.

QUIZ

1. How many types of bird are there?
2. What is the largest order of birds called?
3. What are feathers made of?
4. What shape is a hunting bird's beak?

Answers:
1. Over 9000
2. The Passeriformes order
3. Keratin 4. Hooked

306
Birds lay eggs. It would be impossible for birds to carry their developing young inside their bodies like mammals do – they would be too heavy to fly.

▼ The egg protects the growing chick and provides it with food. While the young develop, the parent birds, such as this common eider, keep the eggs safe and warm. This is called incubation.

Big and small

307 The world's largest bird is the ostrich. This long-legged bird stands up to 2.75 metres tall and weighs up to 115 kilograms – twice as much as an average adult human. Males are slightly larger than females. The ostrich lives mainly on the grasslands of Africa where it feeds on plant material such as leaves, flowers and seeds.

▶ This male ostrich is looking after his chicks. Females are smaller than males and have brown feathers.

308 The bee hummingbird is the world's smallest bird. Its body, including its tail, is about 5 centimetres long and it weighs only 2 grams – about the same as a small spoonful of rice. It lives on Caribbean islands, particularly Cuba, and feeds on flower nectar like other hummingbirds.

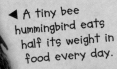
◀ A tiny bee hummingbird eats half its weight in food every day.

309 The heaviest flying bird is the great bustard. The male weighs about 12 kilograms, although the female is slightly smaller. The bustard is a strong flier, but spends much of its life on the ground.

310 Wilson's storm petrel is the smallest seabird in the world. Only 16–19 centimetres long, this petrel hops over the surface of the water snatching up tiny sea creatures to eat. It is very common over the Atlantic, Indian and Antarctic Oceans.

311 **The wandering albatross has the longest wings of any bird.** When outstretched, they can measure as much as 3.6 metres from tip to tip. The albatross spends most of its life in the air. It flies over the oceans, snatching fish and squid from the water's surface.

▲ The wandering albatross only comes to land at breeding time. It lays its eggs on islands in the South Pacific, South Atlantic and Indian Ocean.

312 **The largest bird of prey is the Andean condor.** A type of vulture, this bird measures about 110 centimetres in length and weighs up to 12 kilograms. It soars over the Andes Mountains of South America, hunting for food such as the remains of sheep, cows and llamas.

▶ Andean condors often perch in tall trees and on cliffs.

313 **One of the smallest birds of prey is the collared falconet.** This little bird, which lives in India and Southeast Asia, is only about 17 centimetres long. It hunts insects and other small birds.

▶ The collared falconet lives in forests. Its small size helps it to fly quickly between trees.

Fast movers

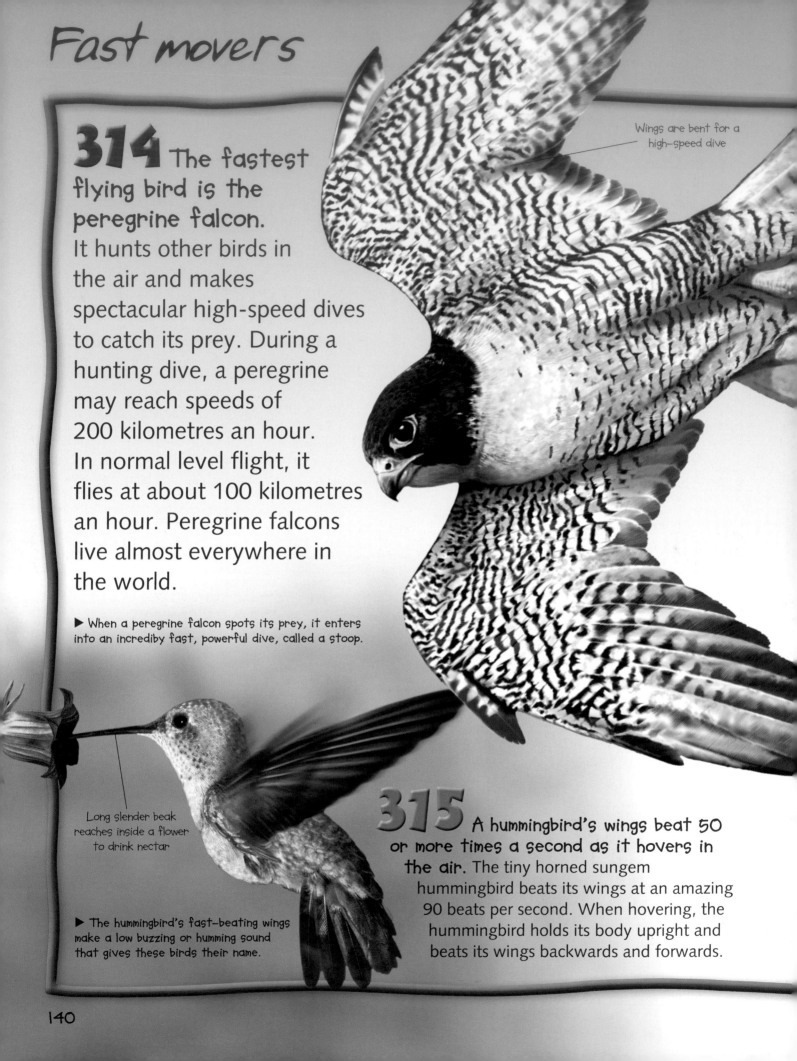

Wings are bent for a high-speed dive

314 The fastest flying bird is the peregrine falcon. It hunts other birds in the air and makes spectacular high-speed dives to catch its prey. During a hunting dive, a peregrine may reach speeds of 200 kilometres an hour. In normal level flight, it flies at about 100 kilometres an hour. Peregrine falcons live almost everywhere in the world.

▶ When a peregrine falcon spots its prey, it enters into an incrediby fast, powerful dive, called a stoop.

Long slender beak reaches inside a flower to drink nectar

▶ The hummingbird's fast-beating wings make a low buzzing or humming sound that gives these birds their name.

315 A hummingbird's wings beat 50 or more times a second as it hovers in the air. The tiny horned sungem hummingbird beats its wings at an amazing 90 beats per second. When hovering, the hummingbird holds its body upright and beats its wings backwards and forwards.

Large, fan-shaped tail

316
Ducks and geese are also fast fliers. Many of them can fly at speeds of more than 65 kilometres an hour. The red-breasted merganser and the common eider duck can fly at up to 100 kilometres an hour.

▲ The male common eider has a distinctive patch of green feathers on the back of its neck.

317
The swift spends nearly all its life in the air and rarely comes to land. After leaving its nest, a young swift can fly up to 500,000 kilometres, and may not come to land again for two years. The common swift has been recorded flying at 112 kilometres an hour.

Swifts have long, slim wings that are perfect for their life in the air

▲ The swift can eat, drink, catch prey and mate on the wing.

318
The greater roadrunner is a fast mover on land. It runs at speeds of up to 27 kilometres an hour as it hunts for insects, lizards and birds' eggs to eat. It can fly but seems to prefer running or walking.

FEED THE BIRDS!

You will need:
225g of fat (suet, lard or dripping)
500g of seeds, nuts, biscuit crumbs, cake and other scraps   a piece of string
Ask an adult for help. Melt the fat, and mix it with the seeds and scraps. Pour it into an old yogurt pot and leave it to cool and harden. Remove the 'cake' and make a hole through it. Push the string through the hole and knot one end. Hang it from a tree, and watch as birds flock to eat it.

Superb swimmers

319 Penguins are the best swimmers and divers in the bird world. They live mostly in and around the Antarctic, at the very south of the world. They spend most of their lives in water, where they catch fish and tiny animals called krill to eat, but they do come to land to breed. Their wings act as strong flippers to push them through the water, and their tail and webbed feet help them to steer. Penguins sometimes get around on land by sliding over ice on their tummies!

▼ King penguins regularly dive to around 50 metres, but will sometimes go as deep as 300 metres, especially when food is scarce.

320 The gentoo penguin is one of the fastest swimming birds. It can swim at up to 36 kilometres an hour – faster than most people can run! Mostly, though, penguins probably swim at about 5 to 10 kilometres an hour.

▶ Gentoos race to shore then leap onto land using the surf to help them 'fly'.

321 The gannet makes an amazing dive from a height of 30 metres above the sea to catch fish. This seabird spots its prey as it soars above the ocean. Then with wings swept back and neck and beak held straight out in front, the gannet plunges like a dive-bomber. It enters the water, seizes its prey and surfaces a few seconds later.

▲ As a gannet plunges into water it must keep its eyes focused on its fast-moving prey.

QUIZ

1. Where do penguins breed – on land or in the water?
2. How fast can a gentoo penguin swim?
3. How deep do king penguins regularly dive?
4. From how high does a gannet dive?

Answers:
1. On land
2. Up to 36 kilometres an hour
3. Around 50 metres 4. 30 metres

143

Looking good

322 At the start of the breeding season male birds try to attract females. Some do this by showing off their feathers. Others perform special displays. The male peacock has a train of colourful feathers. When females come near, he spreads his tail, displaying the beautiful eye-like markings. He shakes the feathers to get the females' attention.

▲ A male peacock displays his beautiful feathers. Females tend to choose males with the most attractive feathers and complicated patterns.

323 The male nightingale sings his tuneful song to attract females. Courtship is the main reason why birds sing, although some may sing at other times of year. A female nightingale chooses a male for his song rather than his looks.

324 The male bowerbird attracts a mate by making a structure of twigs called a bower. He spends many hours making it attractive, by decorating it with berries, flowers and other objects. Females choose the males with the prettiest bowers. After mating, the female makes a nest for her eggs. The male's bower is no longer needed.

◄ The floor of this bird's bower is decorated with stones and plastic objects left behind by people.

326

The male roller performs a special display flight to impress his mate. Starting high in the air, he tumbles and rolls down to the ground while the female watches from a perch. Rollers are brightly coloured insect-eating birds.

◄ A dazzling display by the male will hopefully impress a female blue bird of paradise.

327

Male cocks-of-the-rock dance to attract mates. Some of the most brightly coloured birds in the world, they gather in groups and leap up and down to show off their plumage to admiring females. They live in the South American rainforest.

▼ Male cocks-of-the-rock fight to win a female's attention.

325

The blue bird of paradise hangs upside-down to show off his feathers. As he hangs, his tail feathers spread out and he swings backwards and forwards while making a special call to attract the attention of females. Most birds of paradise live in New Guinea. All the males have beautiful plumage, but females are much plainer.

145

Night birds

328 The barn owl is adapted for hunting at night. Its large eyes are sensitive to dim light. Its ears can pinpoint the tiniest sound and help it to find prey. The fluffy edges of the owl's feathers soften the sound of wing beats so it can swoop silently.

▼ With its pale feathers, the barn owl is a ghostly night-time hunter.

The wings are held high as the bird reaches to grab its prey

329 Some birds, such as the poorwill, hunt insects at night when there is less competition for prey. The poorwill sleeps during the day and wakes up at dusk to start hunting. As it flies, it opens its beak very wide and snaps moths out of the air.

An owl's clawed feet are called talons

330 Like bats, the oilbird of South America uses sounds to help it fly in darkness. As it flies, it makes clicking noises that bounce off obstacles in the caves in which it lives, such as the cave walls, which help the bird find its way. At night, the oilbird leaves the caves to feed on the fruits of palm trees.

The tail is tipped forwards to slow the bird as it lands

► There are fewer than 200 kakapos alive in the world.

331 **The kakapo is the only parrot that is active at night.** During the day the kakapo sleeps in a burrow or under a rock, and at night it comes out to eat fruit, berries and leaves. It cannot fly, but it can climb up into trees using its beak and feet. The kakapo only lives on a few islands off the coast of New Zealand.

332 **Unlike most birds, the kiwi has a good sense of smell that helps it find food at night.** Using the nostrils at the tip of its long beak, the kiwi sniffs out worms and other creatures hiding in the soil. It plunges its beak into the ground to reach its prey.

QUIZ

1. What's special about the barn owl's feathers?
2. Can the kakapo fly?
3. Where are the kiwi's nostrils?

Answers:
1. They have fluffy edges
2. No 3. At the end of its beak

► The kiwi cannot fly. It is active at night, hunting for prey with its long, slender bill.

Home sweet home

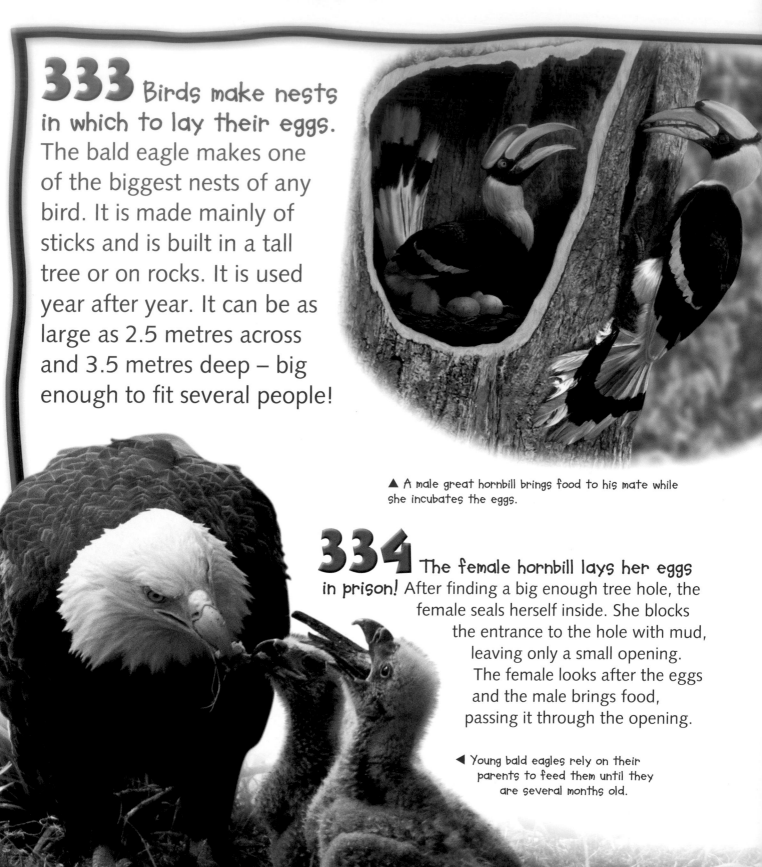

333 Birds make nests in which to lay their eggs. The bald eagle makes one of the biggest nests of any bird. It is made mainly of sticks and is built in a tall tree or on rocks. It is used year after year. It can be as large as 2.5 metres across and 3.5 metres deep – big enough to fit several people!

▲ A male great hornbill brings food to his mate while she incubates the eggs.

334 The female hornbill lays her eggs in prison! After finding a big enough tree hole, the female seals herself inside. She blocks the entrance to the hole with mud, leaving only a small opening. The female looks after the eggs and the male brings food, passing it through the opening.

◄ Young bald eagles rely on their parents to feed them until they are several months old.

▼ A male weaver bird often builds his nest above water. He may build more than one nest, because he can have several mates.

② Then he makes a roof, and an entrance so he can get inside

③ When it's finished, the long entrance helps to provide a safe shelter for the eggs

① The male weaver bird twists strips of leaves around a branch or twig

335
The male weaver bird makes a nest from grass, stems and leaves. He knots and weaves the pieces together to make a long nest, which hangs from the branch of a tree. The nest makes a warm, cosy home for the eggs and young, and is also very hard for any predator to get into.

336
The malleefowl makes a temperature-controlled nest mound. It is made of plants covered with sand. As the plants rot, the inside of the mound gets warmer. The eggs are laid in the sides of the mound. The male keeps a check on the temperature with his beak. If the mound cools, he adds sand. If it gets too hot he makes some openings to let warmth out.

337
The cuckoo doesn't make a nest at all — she lays her eggs in the nests of other birds! She lays up to 12 eggs, all in different nests. The owner of the nest is called the host bird. The female cuckoo removes one of the host bird's eggs before laying one of her own, so the number in the nest remains the same.

338
The cave swiftlet makes a nest from its own saliva or spit. It uses the spit as glue to make a cup-shaped nest of feathers and grass.

Great travellers

339 The Canada goose spends summer in the Arctic and flies south in winter. This regular journey is called a migration. In summer, the Arctic blooms and there is food for the geese to eat while they rear their young. In autumn, when the weather turns colder, they migrate to warmer climates farther south. This means the bird gets warmer weather all year round.

Arctic

Southern North America

▶ Canada geese fly southwards before breeding.

▶ The Arctic tern travels farther than any other bird and sees more hours of daylight each year than any other creature.

Arctic

340 The Arctic tern makes one of the longest migrations of any bird. It breeds in the Arctic during the northern summer. Then, as winter approaches, the tern makes the long journey south to the Antarctic – a trip of some 15,000 kilometres – where it catches the southern summer. The tern gets the benefit of long daylight hours for feeding all year round.

Antarctic

▼ Some flocks of Canada geese make journeys of 1500 kilometres.

Migrating birds can use landmarks, the position of the Sun when it sets and even the Earth's magnetic field to help them navigate.

Arctic tundra

Southern South America

▲ American golden plovers make some of the longest journeys of any animal.

341 Every autumn, the American golden plover flies up to 12,800 kilometres from North to South America. It breeds on the North American tundra where it feasts on the insects that fill the air during the brief Arctic summer. When summer is over the plover flies to the grasslands of southern South America for the winter. This means it has plentiful food supplies all year round.

Desert dwellers

342 The elf owl makes its nest in a hole in a desert cactus. This prickly, uncomfortable home helps to keep the owl's eggs safe from predators that do not want to struggle through the cactus' spines.

▶ The elf owl is one of the smallest owls in the world and is only about 14 centimetres long. It lives in desert areas in the southwest USA.

I DON'T BELIEVE IT!

The lammergeier vulture drops bones onto rocks to smash them. It then eats the soft marrow and even splinters of bone. Acids in the bird's stomach can digest the bone.

343 Desert birds may have to travel long distances to find water. This is not always possible for chicks. To solve this problem, the male sandgrouse has feathers on his tummy that act like sponges to hold water. He soaks his feathers, and then flies back to his young, which gulp down the water that he's brought.

◀ The sandgrouse lives throughout Asia, often in semi-desert areas.

152

344 Many desert birds have very light, sandy-brown feathers to blend with their surroundings. The cream-coloured courser lives in deserts in Africa and Asia. It searches for prey on the ground, as when it flies, the black-and-white pattern on the underside of its wings makes it easier for predators to spot.

◀ A cactus wren rarely needs to drink water. It can get most of what it needs from its food.

345 The lappet-faced vulture scavenges for its food. It glides over the deserts of Africa and the Middle East, searching for dead animals. The vulture attacks a carcass with its strong hooked bill. Its head and neck are bare so it does not have to clean its feathers after feeding from a messy carcass.

346 The cactus wren eats cactus fruits and berries. This little bird hops among the spines of cactus plants in search of juicy morsels. It also catches insects, small lizards and frogs. Cactus wrens live in the southwestern USA.

▼ The lappet-faced vulture is the largest vulture in Africa. It is strong enough to fight off other birds and even mammals such as jackals, and its large beak can rip through skin and muscle.

staying safe

347 Guillemots find that there is safety in numbers. Thousands of these birds live together on clifftops and rocks. They do not build nests but simply lay their eggs on the rock or bare earth. Most land hunters cannot reach the birds on these rocks, and any flying predators are soon driven away by a mass of screeching, pecking birds.

▼ A large breeding colony of guillemots takes up almost every available bit of nesting space on a cliff face.

I DON'T BELIEVE IT!

The guillemot's egg has one end more pointed than the other. This means that the egg rolls in a circle if it is knocked, and does not fall off the cliff.

348 **Birds have clever ways of hiding themselves from predators.** The tawny frogmouth is an Australian bird that hunts at night. During the day, it rests in trees where its brownish, mottled feathers make it hard to see. If the bird senses danger it stretches itself, with its beak pointing upwards, so that it looks almost exactly like a broken branch or tree stump.

349 **If a predator comes too close to her young, the female killdeer leads it away using a clever trick.** She moves away from the nest, which is made on the ground, making sure the predator has noticed her. She then starts to drag one wing as though she is injured and is easy prey. When she has lead the predator far enough away, the killdeer suddenly flies away.

◀ Tawny frogmouths can blend in well, despite being large birds. They can grow to 50 centimetres long.

▶ A female killdeer imitates an injured wing to lead a predator away from her nest.

Amazing eggs

350
A bird's egg protects the developing chick inside. The yellow yolk in the egg provides the chick with food. Layers of egg white, called albumen, cushion the chick and keep it warm, and also supply it with food. The hard shell keeps everything safe. The shell is porous – it allows air in and out so that the chick can breathe. The parent birds incubate the egg in the nest.

351
The number of eggs laid in a clutch varies from one to more than 20. A clutch is the name for the number of eggs that a bird lays in one go. The number of clutches per year also changes from bird to bird. The grey partridge lays one of the biggest clutches, with an average of 15 to 19 eggs. The emperor penguin lays just one egg a year.

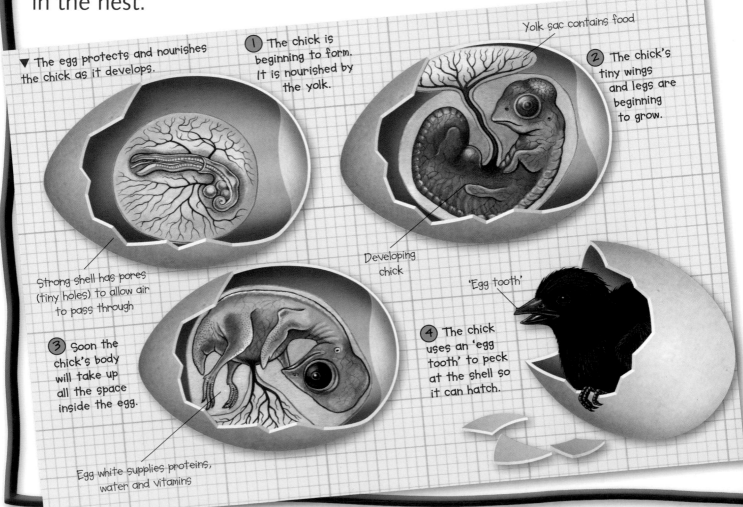

▼ The egg protects and nourishes the chick as it develops.

Strong shell has pores (tiny holes) to allow air to pass through

① The chick is beginning to form. It is nourished by the yolk.

Yolk sac contains food

② The chick's tiny wings and legs are beginning to grow.

Developing chick

③ Soon the chick's body will take up all the space inside the egg.

Egg white supplies proteins, water and vitamins

'Egg tooth'

④ The chick uses an 'egg tooth' to peck at the shell so it can hatch.

352 The ostrich egg is the biggest in the world. It weighs about 1.5 kilograms – an average hen's egg weighs only about 50 grams. The shell of the ostrich egg is very strong, measuring up to 2 millimetres thick. A female ostrich can lay up to 30 enormous eggs at a time. However, the ostrich egg is actually the smallest when compared to the size of the parent bird.

◄ An ostrich egg measures 16 centimetres in length.

353 The smallest egg in the world is laid by the bee hummingbird. The delicate egg is laid in a cup-shaped nest of cobwebs and plants. It weighs about 0.3 grams. The bird itself weighs only 2 grams.

ACTUAL SIZE

◄ The bee hummingbird egg is just 6 millimetres in length.

354 The kiwi lays an egg a quarter of her own size. The egg weighs 420 grams – the kiwi itself weighs only 1.7 kilograms. This is equivalent to a new human baby weighing 17.5 kilograms – most weigh about 3.5 kilograms.

355 The great spotted woodpecker incubates its egg for only ten days. This is one of the shortest incubation periods of any bird. The longest is of the wandering albatross, which incubates its eggs for up to 82 days.

► A female great spotted woodpecker feeds a juicy caterpillar to her hungry chick. Once a chick has hatched it needs a lot of food.

QUIZ

1. Which part of the egg cushions the chick?
2. How many eggs a year does the emperor penguin lay?
3. How much does the bee hummingbird's egg weigh?
4. For how long does the wandering albatross incubate its eggs?

Answers:
1. The egg white (albumen)
2. One 3. 0.3 grams
4. Up to 82 days

Hunters and scavengers

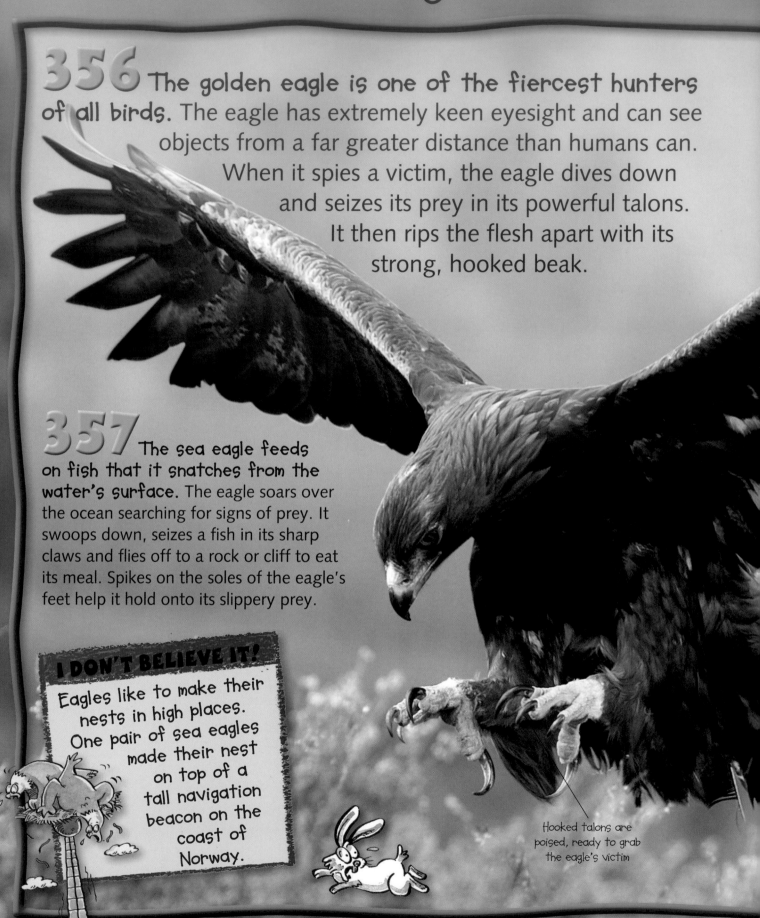

356 The golden eagle is one of the fiercest hunters of all birds. The eagle has extremely keen eyesight and can see objects from a far greater distance than humans can. When it spies a victim, the eagle dives down and seizes its prey in its powerful talons. It then rips the flesh apart with its strong, hooked beak.

357 The sea eagle feeds on fish that it snatches from the water's surface. The eagle soars over the ocean searching for signs of prey. It swoops down, seizes a fish in its sharp claws and flies off to a rock or cliff to eat its meal. Spikes on the soles of the eagle's feet help it hold onto its slippery prey.

I DON'T BELIEVE IT!

Eagles like to make their nests in high places. One pair of sea eagles made their nest on top of a tall navigation beacon on the coast of Norway.

Hooked talons are poised, ready to grab the eagle's victim

A single wing feather can be 35 to 50 centimetres long

◄ The golden eagle can soar for hours, searching for prey such as rabbits and other birds.

358 The raven is one of the biggest songbirds and a powerful hunter. It grows up to 63 centimetres long, has a strong beak and can run fast on the ground as well as fly. Rats and mice are its main prey, but it can even kill a creature as large as a rabbit. Ravens also scavenge, eating animals that are already dead or the kills of other hunters.

Tail feathers are unusually long – up to 35 centimetres

► Ravens look like crows, but their beaks are bigger and stronger.

Caring for the young

359 Emperor penguins have the worst breeding conditions of any bird. They lay eggs and rear their young on the Antarctic ice. The female penguin lays one egg at the start of the Antarctic winter. She returns to the sea, leaving her partner to incubate it on his feet. The egg is covered by a flap of the male's skin, which keeps it warm.

360 Hawks and falcons look after their young and bring them food for many weeks. Their chicks are born blind and helpless. They are totally dependent on their parents for food and protection until they grow large enough to hunt for themselves.

▶ When the chick hatches, the female penguin returns while the hungry male finds food. Emperor penguin chicks sit on their parents' feet to keep off the frozen ground.

▼ Peregrine falcon parents normally care for two to four chicks at a time.

361 Pigeons feed their young on 'pigeon milk'. This special liquid is made in the lining of part of the bird's throat, called the crop. The young birds are fed on this for the first few days of their lives and then start to eat seeds and other solid food.

362

Some birds, such as ducks and geese, are able to move around as soon as they hatch. Ducklings follow the first moving thing they see – usually their mother. This is called imprinting. It is a form of learning that can happen only in the first few hours of an animal's life. It ensures that the young birds stay close to their mother.

▼ These mallard chicks stand a greater chance of survival by staying close to their mother.

363

Young birds must learn their songs from adults. A young bird such as a chaffinch is born being able to make sounds. But, like a human baby learning to speak, it has to learn the chaffinch song by listening to its parents and practising.

364

Swans carry their young on their back as they swim. This allows the parent bird to move fast without having to wait for the young, called cygnets, to keep up. When the cygnets are riding on the parent bird's back they are safe from predators.

▼ A female mute swan and cygnets. Both parents take turns to care for the young.

Deep in the jungle

365 Birds of paradise are among the most colourful of all rainforest birds. The males have brilliant plumage and decorative feathers. There are about 42 different kinds and all live in the forests of New Guinea and northeast Australia. Fruit is their main source of food, but some feed on insects.

366 The scarlet macaw is one of the largest parrots in the world. It is an incredible 85 centimetres long, including its impressive tail, and lives in the South American rainforest. It moves in large flocks that screech as they fly from tree to tree, feeding on fruit and leaves.

◄ Parrots, such as the scarlet macaw, have hooked beaks that they use to crack nuts, open seeds and tear at fruit.

367 The junglefowl is the wild ancestor of the farmyard chicken. This colourful bird lives in the rainforests of Southeast Asia, where it feeds on seeds and insects.

► Hoatzins often live in small groups, and share the care of their chicks.

368 The hoatzin builds its nest overhanging water. If its chicks are in danger from predators they can escape by dropping into the water and swimming to safety. This strange bird with its ragged crest lives in the Amazon rainforest.

369 The Congo peafowl was only discovered in 1936. It lives in the dense rainforest of West Africa and is rarely seen. The male bird has beautiful glossy feathers of green, violet-blue and red, while the female is mostly brown and green.

▼ Harpy eagles perch on high branches to get a good view of the forest below.

370 The harpy eagle is the world's largest eagle. It is about 90 centimetres long and has huge feet and long, sharp claws. It feeds on rainforest animals such as monkeys and sloths.

◄ Quetzals can perch without moving a muscle, making themselves hard to spot in the rainforest.

371 The male resplendant quetzal has magnificent tail feathers, which are up to 90 centimetres long. This beautiful bird lives in the rainforests of Mexico and South America. It was worshipped as a sacred bird by the ancient Mayan and Aztec people.

Flightless birds

372 The fast-running emu is the largest bird native to Australia. Like the ostrich it cannot fly, but it can run at speeds of up to 50 kilometres an hour. Most flightless birds need speed to avoid being caught by predators. They have long legs, packed with muscles. Ostriches and emus can also deliver a mighty kick if they are scared.

▲ Emus can only run at top speed for a short time. They are hunted by wild dogs, eagles and crocodiles.

I DON'T BELIEVE IT!

One rhea egg is the equivalent in size to about 12 hen's eggs. It has long been a tasty feast for local people.

Very powerful upper leg muscles

Extra flexible ankles

▶ The ostrich is the world's fastest two-legged runner. It is specially adapted for speed, and can run at up to 70 kilometres an hour.

Penguins can waddle, run and jump, and are very strong swimmers

Kiwis rely on the cover of darkness, not speed, to stay safe

Roadrunners can reach speeds of 32 kilometres an hour, and they can also fly a little

▲ There are about 40 different types of flightless birds alive today, which have various ways of staying safe.

373
The speedy rhea lives on the grassy plains of South America. In the breeding season, males fight to gather a flock of females. Once he has his flock, the winning male digs a nest. Each of the females lays her eggs in this nest. The male incubates them, and looks after the chicks until they are about six months old.

▲ The rhea can sprint faster than a horse, reaching speeds of up to 50 kilometres an hour.

Long, strong legs

Bendy two-toed feet

374
Cassowaries are flightless birds that live in the rainforests of Australia and New Guinea. There are three species – all are large birds with long, strong legs and big, sharp-clawed feet. On the cassowary's head is a large horny crest, called a casque. Experts are not sure why cassowaries have casques, but they may be useful in making, and hearing, low booming calls that can be heard in the dense forest.

On the river

375 Kingfishers live close to rivers, where they hunt for fish. At breeding time, a pair of birds tunnels into the riverbank, using their strong beaks. They prepare a nesting chamber at the end of the long tunnel. Here the female can safely lay up to eight eggs. Both parents look after the eggs, and feed the chicks when they hatch.

▶ A kingfisher plunges into the water, grabbing a fish in its dagger-like beak.

▼ Ospreys are also known as 'fish hawks'. As they dive into the water, they keep the prey in their sights.

376 The osprey is a bird of prey that feeds mainly on fish. This bird is found almost all over the world near rivers and lakes. It watches for prey from the air then plunges into the water with its feet held out in front. Special spikes on the soles of its feet help it hold onto its slippery catch.

377 The pelican collects fish in the big pouch that hangs beneath its long beak. When the pelican pushes its beak into the water the pouch stretches and fills with water, scooping up fish. When the pelican lifts its head up, the water drains out of the pouch leaving the food behind.

▲ A pelican's massive pouch works like a fishing net to trap prey.

378 The jacana can walk on water! It has amazingly long toes that spread the bird's weight over a large area. This allows it to walk on floating lily pads as it hunts for food such as insects. Jacanas can also swim and dive. There are eight different types of jacana, also called lilytrotters.

379 The heron catches fish and other creatures such as insects and frogs. This long-legged bird stands on the shore or in shallow water and grabs its prey with a swift thrust of its sharp beak.

380 A small bird called the dipper is well-adapted to river life. It usually lives around fast-flowing streams and can swim and dive well. It can even walk along the bottom of a stream, snapping up prey such as insects and other small creatures. There are five different types of dipper and they live in North and South America, Asia and Europe.

▶ An African jacana feeds from water lettuce on the head of a hippopotamus.

Finding food

381 The woodpecker uses its strong beak to bore into tree trunks and catch insects. The bird holds on to a tree trunk using its strong feet and sharp claws. Its stiff tail feathers also provide support. It hammers into the trunk, disturbing wood-boring insects that live beneath the bark. The woodpecker quickly snaps up the escaping insects.

◄ Woodpeckers also use their beaks to make nest holes in tree trunks, like this red-bellied woodpecker.

I DON'T BELIEVE IT!

The hummingbird has to eat lots of nectar to get enough energy to survive. If a human were to work as hard as a hummingbird, he or she would need to eat three times their weight in potatoes each day.

382 The antbird keeps watch over army ants as they march through the forest.

The bird flies just ahead of the ants and perches on a low branch. It then pounces on the insects, spiders and other small creatures that try to escape from the column of ants. Some antbirds also eat the ants. Antbirds live in North and South America.

▲ Ocellated antbirds have a 'tooth' at the tip of the beak, for crushing insects.

383 The honeyguide bird uses the honey badger to help it get to its food.

Found in parts of Africa and Asia, the honeyguide feeds on bee grubs and honey. It is not strong enough to break into bees' nests, so it leads the honey badger towards them. When the honey badger smashes into the nest, the honeyguide can also eat its fill.

384 The hummingbird feeds on flower nectar.

Nectar is a sweet liquid made by flowers to attract pollinating insects. It is not always easy for birds to reach, but the hummingbird is able to hover in front of the flower while it sips the nectar using its long tongue.

▲ Colourful flowers and sweet perfumes attract nectar feeders, such as hummingbirds.

Winter birds

385 The coldest places on Earth are the Arctic and the Antarctic. The Arctic is at the most northern point of the Earth, and the Antarctic is at the far south. The snowy owl is one of the largest birds in the Arctic. Its white feathers help to camouflage it in the snow.

Dark bars on a female's feathers help her to hide when she is nesting among snowy rocks

386 Penguins have a thick layer of fat just under their skin to help protect them from the cold. Their feathers are waterproof and very tightly packed for warmth. Penguins live mainly in Antarctica, but some live in parts of South Africa, South America and Australia.

▶ Snowy owls ambush their prey, approaching with almost silent wing-beats.

387 In winter, the ptarmigan has white feathers to help it hide from predators in the Arctic snow. But in summer its white plumage would make it very easy to spot, so the ptarmigan moults and grows brown and grey feathers instead.

Summer plumage

Winter plumage

◀ Rock ptarmigans are stocky birds that feed on plants at ground level.

▲ Bewick swans care for their young throughout their first winter, and sometimes for a second winter too.

388 The Bewick swan lays its eggs and rears its young on the tundra of the Arctic. The female bird makes a nest on the ground and lays up to five eggs. Both parents care for the young. In autumn the family travels south to warmer lands.

389 Sheathbills are scavengers and will eat almost anything they can find. These large white birds live on islands close to the Antarctic. They do catch fish but they also search the beaches for any dead animals. They will also snatch weak or dying young from seals and penguins.

▼ A sheathbill tries to steal food from a gentoo penguin feeding its chick.

390 The snow bunting breeds on Arctic islands and farther north than any other bird. The female makes a nest of grasses, moss and lichens on the ground. She lays four to eight eggs and both parents help to care for the young.

Snowy owls have a wingspan of about 130 centimetres

QUIZ

1. Which is situated at the far south of the world – the Arctic or the Antarctic?
2. Why do penguins have a layer of fat underneath their skin?
3. Where do Bewick swans lay their eggs?

Answers:
1. The Antarctic 2. To protect them from the cold 3. The Arctic tundra

Special beaks

391 The snail kite feeds primarily on water snails, and its curved beak is specially shaped for this diet. When the kite catches a snail, it holds it in one foot while standing on a branch or other perch. It strikes the snail's body with its sharp beak and shakes it from the shell.

▲ The snail kite is a type of hawk that lives in the southern USA, the Caribbean and South America. It is now very rare.

392 The lower half of the skimmer's beak is longer than the upper half. The skimmer flies just above the water with the lower part below the surface. When it comes across a fish, the skimmer snaps the upper part down to trap its prey.

393 The crossbill has a very unusual beak that crosses at the tip. This shape helps the bird to open up the scales of pine cones and remove the seeds that it feeds on.

◄ Male crossbills are red. Females are usually olive green or greenish–yellow, although both have dark brown wings and tail.

172

► There are sieve-like plates on the edges of a flamingo's beak. These plates help to trap the food that the bird eats.

394 The flamingo uses its beak to filter food from shallow water. It stands in the water with its head down and its beak beneath the surface. Water flows into the beak and is pushed out again by the flamingo's large tongue. Tiny animals and plants are trapped – and swallowed.

▼ This female wrybill can use her beak to reach young insects that lurk beneath pebbles.

395 The wrybill is the only bird with a beak that curves to the right. The wrybill is a type of plover that lives in New Zealand. It sweeps its beak over the ground in circles to pick up insects.

396 The toco toucan's beak is about 19 centimetres long. It helps the toucan to reach fruit and berries at the ends of branches. All toucans have large brightly coloured beaks. The different colours and patterns may help them attract mates.

▲ As well as a way of eating fruit, scientists think that a toucan's large beak may help it to lose heat when the bird is too hot.

397 People buying and selling wild birds has led to some species becoming very rare. Some pet birds, such as budgerigars, are bred in captivity but others, such as parrots, are illegally taken from the wild. The hyacinth macaw, which used to be common in South American jungles, is now rare due to people catching it to sell.

► There are fewer than 7000 hyacinth macaws left in the wild.

398 In some parts of the world, people still keep falcons for hunting. The birds are trained to kill animals and bring them back. When the birds are taken out, they wear special hoods to keep them calm. These are removed when the bird is released to chase its prey.

◄ Falconry — the practice of hunting with trained birds of prey — is one of the oldest sports in the world.

399

Many kinds of birds are reared for their eggs and meat. Chickens and their eggs are a major food source in many countries, and turkeys, ducks and geese are also eaten. Some wild birds, such as pheasants, are also used for food.

400

Starlings are common city birds. Huge flocks are often seen roosting on buildings. Starlings originally lived in Europe and Asia but were introduced to other countries. For example, in 1890, 60 starlings were released in New York City, followed by another 40 in 1891. Now starlings are among the most common birds in North America. The starling is very adaptable. It will eat a wide range of foods, and will nest almost anywhere.

▼ A huge flock of starlings such as this in Brighton, UK, makes a spectacular sight. One flock can number up to 100,000 birds.

I DON'T BELIEVE IT!

Urban-living crows drop walnuts amongst traffic. The cars break the shells as they move. The crows wait by crossings, and when the lights change to red, hop into the road to pick up the kernels!

MAMMALS

401 Mammals are warm-blooded animals with a bony skeleton and fur or hair. Being warm-blooded means that a mammal keeps its body at a constant temperature, even if the weather is very cold. The skeleton supports the body and protects the delicate parts inside, such as the heart, lungs and brain. There is one sort of mammal you know very well, it's you!

▼▶ Two western lowland gorillas meet face to face. Gorillas are highly intelligent mammals and close cousins of humans.

Mammal groups

402 There are nearly 5500 different types of mammal. Most mammals have babies that grow inside the mother's body. While a baby mammal grows, a special organ called a placenta supplies it with food and oxygen from the mother's body. These mammals are called placental mammals.

Placental mammals

Placenta

Birth canal

▲ A baby elephant in the womb receives nourishment through the placenta.

403 Not all mammals' young develop inside the mother's body. Two smaller groups of mammals do things differently. Monotremes, such as platypuses and echidnas (spiny anteaters), lay eggs. The platypus lays her eggs in a burrow, but the echidna keeps her single egg in a special pouch in her belly until it is ready to hatch.

► The echidna keeps her egg in a pouch until it hatches after about ten days.

Monotremes

404 Mammal mothers feed their babies on milk from their own bodies. The baby sucks this milk from teats on special mammary glands, also called udders or breasts, on the mother's body. The milk contains all the food the young animal needs to help it grow.

405

Marsupials give birth to tiny young that finish developing in a pouch. A baby kangaroo is only 2 centimetres long when it is born. Tiny, blind and hairless, it makes its own way to the safety of its mother's pouch. Once there, it latches onto a teat in the pouch and begins to feed.

A joey starts life as a tiny undeveloped baby

Marsupials

▲ A baby kangaroo is called a joey. It stays in the pouch for about six months while it grows.

▼ This reindeer uses its eyes, ears and especially nose to sense the world.

406

Most mammals have good senses of sight, smell and hearing. Their senses help them watch out for enemies, find food and keep in touch with each other. For many mammals, smell is their most important sense. Plant-eaters such as rabbits and deer sniff the air to pick up scents of danger, especially those of predators.

I DON'T BELIEVE IT!

Lemmings are very fast breeders. Females can become pregnant at only 14 days old, and they can produce litters of as many as 12 young every month.

Big and small

407 The blue whale is the biggest mammal, and one of the largest animals ever known to have lived. It can measure as long as seven family cars parked end to end, and spends all of its life in the ocean.

ELEPHANT
4 metres tall
▶ Elephants may eat more than 300 kilograms of leaves, twigs and fruit each day.

408 The elephant is the biggest land mammal. There are three kinds of elephant – the African savannah elephant, the African forest elephant, and the Asian. The African savannah elephant is the biggest – a full-grown male may weigh as much as 10 tonnes – more than 100 adult people.

GORILLA
1.75 metres tall

▼ A full-grown male gorilla weighs up to 275 kilograms.

GIRAFFE
5.5 metres tall

▼ The giraffe's height helps it reach juicy leaves at the tops of trees.

409 Gorillas are the biggest primates. Primates are the group of mammals to which chimpanzees and humans belong.

410 The giraffe is the tallest animal, as well as mammal. A male is as tall as three or four people standing on each other's shoulders. Giraffes lives in Africa, south of the Sahara desert.

411 The capybara is the largest rodent. Rodents are the group of mammals that include rats and mice. It lives around ponds, lakes and rivers in South America.

CAPYBARA
1.3 metres long

▲ A well-fed capybara weighs over 70 kilograms.

MOUSE DEER
85 cm long

▲ The mouse deer is just 30 centimetres in height.

412 The tiny mouse deer is the size of a hare. Also know as the chevrotain, it lives in African forests.

413 The smallest mammal is the tiny hog-nosed bat. A full-grown adult weighs less than a teaspoon of rice!

HOG-NOSED BAT
3 centimetres long

▶ The tiny hog-nosed bat is just 2 grams in weight.

Fast movers

414 The cheetah can run faster than any other animal. It can move at about 100 kilometres an hour, but it cannot run this fast for long. The cheetah uses its speed to catch other animals to eat. It creeps towards its prey until it is only about 100 metres away. Then it races towards it at top speed, ready for the final attack.

415 The pronghorn is slower than the cheetah, but can run for longer. It can keep up a speed of 70 kilometres an hour for about ten minutes.

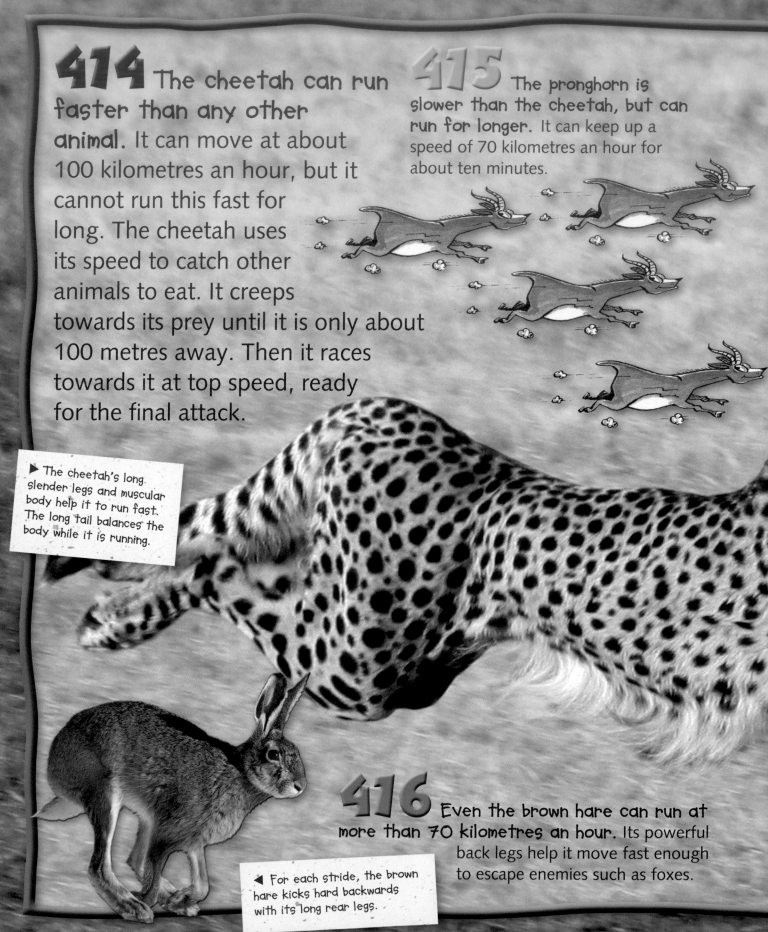

▶ The cheetah's long slender legs and muscular body help it to run fast. The long tail balances the body while it is running.

416 Even the brown hare can run at more than 70 kilometres an hour. Its powerful back legs help it move fast enough to escape enemies such as foxes.

◀ For each stride, the brown hare kicks hard backwards with its long rear legs.

SPEED DEMONS!

Ask an adult to measure how far in metres you can run in 10 seconds. Multiply this by 6, and then times the answer by 60 to find out how many metres you can run in an hour. If you divide this by 1000 you will get your speed in kilometres per hour. You will find it will be far less than the cheetah's 100 kilometres an hour!

◄ The red kangaroo can leap 9 or 10 metres in a single bound.

417 The red kangaroo is a champion jumper. It can leap along at 40 kilometres an hour or more. The kangaroo needs to be able to travel fast. It lives in the dry desert lands of Australia and often has to journey long distances to find grass to eat and water to drink.

Swimmers and divers

418 Most swimming mammals have flippers and fins instead of legs. Their bodies have become sleek and streamlined to help them move through the water easily. Seals and sea lions have large, paddle-like flippers that they can use to drag themselves along on land, as well as for swimming power in water. Whales never come to land. They swim by moving their tails up and down and using their front flippers to steer.

▲ The humpback has the largest flippers of any whale, at 5 metres long.

419 The killer whale can reach a speed of 55 kilometres an hour. A fierce hunter, it uses its speed to chase fast-swimming prey such as squid, fish and seals. It sometimes hunts in groups and will even attack other whales. Killer whales live in all the world's oceans. Despite their name, they are the largest of the dolphin family. They grow up to 10 metres long and weigh as much as 9 tonnes.

◀ Killer whales often leap clear of the water, an action known as breaching.

▼ A mother and baby Weddell seal. The Weddell is a big seal – 3.5 metres long and half a tonne in weight.

420 The Weddell seal can dive deeper than any other seal. It goes down to depths of 750 metres or more in its search for cod and other fish. This seal can stay underwater for a long while, and dives of more than an hour have been timed. It lives in the icy waters of Antarctica, and its body is covered with a thick layer of fatty blubber that helps to keep it warm.

Fliers and gliders

421 Bats are the only true flying mammals. They zoom through the air on wings made of skin. These are attached to the sides of their body and supported by specially adapted, extra-long bones of the arms and hands and fingers. Bats generally hunt at night. During the day they hang upside down by their feet from a branch or cave ledge. Their wings are neatly folded at their sides or around their body.

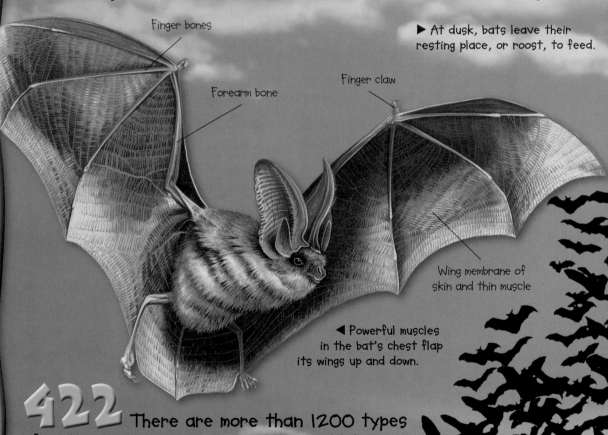

Finger bones

Forearm bone

Finger claw

▶ At dusk, bats leave their resting place, or roost, to feed.

Wing membrane of skin and thin muscle

◀ Powerful muscles in the bat's chest flap its wings up and down.

422 There are more than 1200 types of bat. They live in most parts of the world, but not in colder areas. Bats feed on many different sorts of food. Most common are the insect-eating bats, which snatch their prey from the air while in flight. Others feast on pollen and nectar from flowers. Flesh-eating bats catch fish, birds, lizards and frogs.

423 Flying lemurs don't really fly – they just glide from tree to tree. They can glide distances of up to 100 metres with the help of flaps of skin at the sides of the body. When the flying lemur takes off from a branch it holds its limbs out, stretching the skin flaps so that they act like a parachute.

▼ The skin flaps of the flying lemur, or colugo, are not only along the sides, but also between the rear legs and tail.

I DON'T BELIEVE IT!

The vampire bat is a blood-drinker! It consumes about 26 litres of blood a year – about the total blood supply of five human beings!

424 Other gliding mammals are the flying squirrels and gliders. All can glide from tree to tree, like the flying lemur, with the help of flaps of skin at the sides of the body. Flying squirrels live in North America and parts of Asia. Gliders are a type of possum and live in Australia and New Guinea.

Life in snow and ice

425 The polar bear is the biggest land predator. This Arctic hunter can run fast, swim well and even dive under the ice to hunt its main prey – seals. It also catches seabirds and land animals such as the Arctic hare and reindeer.

▶ The polar bear's thick, white fur helps to keep it warm – even the soles of its feet are furry.

426 Caribou, also known as reindeer, feed in Arctic lands. The land around the Arctic Ocean is called the tundra. In the short summer, plenty of plants grow, the caribou eat their fill and give birth to their young. When summer is over, the caribou trek up to 1000 kilometres south to spend the winter in forests.

427 Some Arctic animals such as the Arctic hare and the ermine, or stoat, change colour. In winter these animals have white fur, which helps them hide among the snow. In summer, when white fur would make them very easy to spot, their coats turn brown.

◀ Reindeer scrape and nose into snow to find plants to eat.

428 The Arctic ground squirrel digs its own burrow system to shelter in, or renovates an old, unoccupied set of burrows. It lines the main nest area with dry grass, moss and thin stems. Here it hibernates for half the year or more – from August to the following April.

429 The leopard seal is one of the fiercest hunters in the Antarctic. It lives in the waters around Antarctica and preys on penguins, fish and other seals. There are no land mammals in the Antarctic.

▲ After waking from hibernation, plants, seeds and berries make up the diet of the Arctic ground squirrel.

430 The walrus has tusks that grow as much as one metre long. They are used to drag itself out of water and onto the ice as well as for defending itself against enemies and for display against rival walruses.

431 The musk ox has a long shaggy outer coat to help it survive the Arctic cold. A thick undercoat keeps out the damp. The musk ox eats grass, moss and lichen. In winter it digs through the snow with its hooves to reach its food.

▼ Huge male musk ox head-butt to control the herd.

Creatures of the night

432 Not all mammals are active during the day. Some sleep during daylight and wake up at night. They are nocturnal, and there are many reasons for their habits. Overall there are fewer predators active at night, and it is easier to hide in gloomy undergrowth and dark corners.

433 The aye-aye is a strange tree-dwelling lemur of Madagascar. Like many nocturnal animals it has large eyes to collect as much light as possible. It sleeps by day in a nest of leaves and twigs and searches at night for grubs and other small creatures, using its very long fourth finger to pull them from under bark.

▲ An aye-aye probes into holes in trunks and branches for food.

QUIZ

1. What word describes animals that are active at night?

2. Where does the aye-aye live?

3. What does the red panda eat?

Answers:
1. Nocturnal 2. Madagascar
3. Bamboo shoots, fruit, acorns, insects, birds' eggs

190

434 The red panda is a night feeder. It sleeps during the day, but at night it searches for food such as bamboo shoots, roots, fruit and acorns. It also eats insects, birds' eggs and small animals. In summer, red pandas sometimes wake in the day to climb trees to find fresh leaves to eat.

435 Hyenas usually come out at night to find food. They hunt their own prey and are also scavangers – they feed on the remains of creatures killed by larger hunters. When a lion has eaten its fill, hyenas rush in to grab the remains.

436 Bats hunt at night. Insect feeders, such as the horseshoe bat, manage to find their prey by means of a special kind of animal sonar. The bat makes high-pitched squeaks as it flies. If the waves from these sounds hit an animal, such as a moth, echoes bounce back to the bat. These echoes tell the bat where its prey is.

◄ Hyenas hunt at night using their excellent sense of smell.

Busy builders

437 Beavers build their home by damming a stream with branches, stones and mud. This creates a deep lake where they can make a winter food store and a shelter called a lodge. Once the dam is made, they begin to build the lodge, usually a dome-shaped structure made of sticks and mud.

▶ Beavers repair and strengthen their dam daily. In summer, they feed on twigs, leaves and roots. They collect extra branches and logs to store for winter.

Dam holds back water

438 The beaver is an excellent swimmer. It has a broad flat tail, which acts like a paddle when swimming, and it has webbed feet. It dives well, too, and can stay underwater for 15 minutes or more. To warn others of danger, a beaver may slap the water with its tail as it dives.

439 The harvest mouse makes a nest on grass stems. It winds some strong stems round one another to make a kind of platform. It then weaves softer grass stems into the structure to form a ball-like shape about 10 centimetres across.

▶ The female harvest mouse looks after as many as ten babies in her tennis ball-sized woven nest.

Dry living platform

Underwater entrance to lodge

Incisor teeth gnaw wood

Family life

440 Many mammals live alone, except when they have young, but others live in groups. Wolves live in family groups called packs. The pack is led by an adult female and her mate and may include up to 20 animals.

441 A type of mongoose called a meerkat lives in large groups of up to 30 animals. The group is called a colony and contains several family units of a pair of adults along with their young. The colony lives in a network of underground burrows. The members of the colony guard each other against enemies.

▲ As a pack, wolves can hunt large prey like deer and bison.

▼ Some meerkats watch for danger while others feed.

442 The male elephant seal fights rival males to gather a group of females. This group is called a harem and the male seal defends his females from other males. The group does not stay together for long after mating.

443 Some whales live in families too. Pilot whales, for example, live in groups of 20 or more animals that swim and hunt together. A group may include several adult males and a number of females and their young.

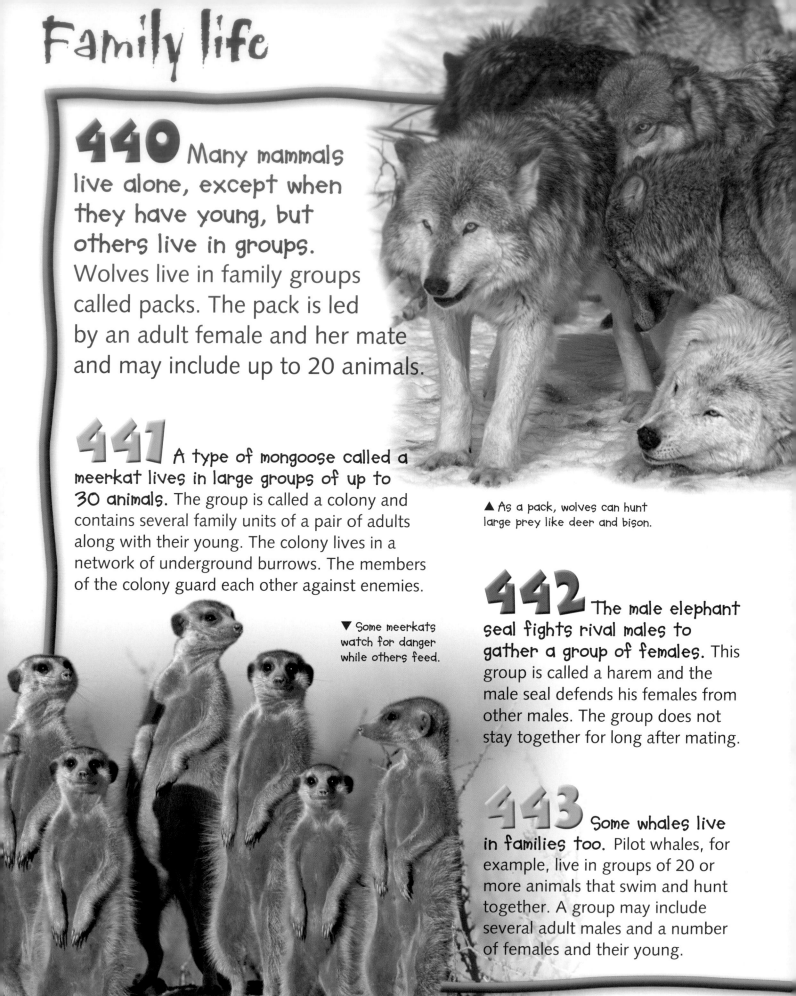

444
Naked mole rats live underground in a colony of animals led by one female. The colony includes about 100 animals and the ruling female, or queen, is the only one that produces young. Other colony members dig burrows to find food for the group, and look after the queen.

445
Lions live in groups called prides. The pride may include one or more adult males, females related to each other, and their young. The average number in a pride is 15. Female young generally stay with the pride of their birth but males must leave before they are full-grown. Lions are unusual in their family lifestyle – most other big cats live alone.

▼ Bonobos are generally peaceful, sharing food with each other.

446
Bonobos (pygmy chimpanzees) live in large groups, known as communities, of 80 or more. These are usually a mix of females, males and young. Within the community certain individuals are close friends and interact more than with others. These groups spend time together looking for food, grooming each other, and resting. Sometimes, the whole community gathers to travel, usually led by one or a few females, or to sleep.

Desert dwellers

447 Many desert animals burrow underground to escape the scorching heat. The North African gerbil stays hidden all day and comes out at night to eat seeds and insects. This gerbil is so well adapted to desert life that it never needs to drink.

▶ The North African gerbil gets all the liquid it needs from its food.

448 The large ears of the fennec fox help it to lose heat from its body. This fox lives in the North African desert. For its size, it has the largest ears of any dog or fox.

449 Pallas's cat lives in the Gobi Desert. It has thick, long fur to keep it warm in the cold Gobi winter. Pallas's cat lives alone, usually in a cave or a burrow, and hunts mice and birds.

▶ The fennec's huge ears can hear prey as tiny as ants.

450 A camel can last for weeks without drinking. It can manage on the liquid it gets from feeding on desert plants. But when it does find some water it drinks as much as 100 litres at one time. It does not store water in its hump, but it can store fat.

451
A kangaroo rat never needs to drink. The kidneys control how much water there is in an animal's body. The kangaroo rat's kidneys are much more efficient than ours. It can even make some of its food into water inside its body!

452
The bactrian camel has thick fur to keep it warm in winter. It lives in the Gobi Desert in Asia where winter weather can be very cold indeed. In summer, the camel's long shaggy fur drops off, leaving the camel almost hairless.

453
The desert hedgehog eats scorpions! It carefully nips off the scorpion's deadly sting before eating. It also eats insects and birds' eggs.

◄ The camel's hump fat is broken down into energy and water.

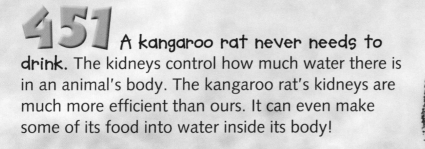

Backbone

Fat in hump

Blood supply

Intestines

Stomach

On the prowl

454 Mammals that hunt and kill other creatures are called carnivores. Examples of carnivores are lions, tigers, wolves and dogs. Meat is a more concentrated food than plants so many carnivores do not have to hunt every day. One kill lasts them for several days.

▶ Most carnivores will hunt creatures smaller than themselves. The lion can more easily catch and kill smaller prey like this zebra foal.

455 The tiger is the biggest cat and an expert hunter. It hunts alone, usually for buffalo, deer and wild pigs. The tiger prefers to creep up on prey without being noticed, rather than chase it. Its stripy coat helps it to hide in long grass. When it is as close as possible, the tiger pounces, clamps its jaws around its victim's throat and suffocates it.

▲ A tiger silently stalks its prey, keeping its body low to the ground to remain unseen and unheard.

FOOD CHAIN

Make your own food chain. Draw a picture of a large carnivore such as a lion and tie it to a piece of string. Then draw a picture of an animal that the lion catches such as a zebra. Hang that from the picture of the lion. Lastly draw a picture of lots of grass and plants (the food of the zebra). Hang that from the picture of the zebra.

456 Bears eat many different foods. They are carnivores but most, except for the polar bear, eat more plant material than meat. Brown bears eat fruit, nuts and insects and even catch fish. In summer, when salmon swim up rivers to lay their eggs, the bears wade into the shallows and hook fish with their huge paws.

457 Hunting dogs hunt in packs. Together, they can bring down a much larger animal. The pack sets off after a herd of plant-eaters such as zebras or gazelles. They try to separate one animal that is perhaps weaker or slower from the rest of the herd.

◄ This young wildebeest has been separated from its herd by a pack of African hunting dogs.

Fighting back

458 Some mammals have special ways of defending themselves from enemies. The nine-banded armadillo has body armour. Bony plates, topped with a layer of horn, cover the armadillo's back, sides and head.

459 The porcupine's body is covered with as many as 30,000 sharp spines. When an enemy approaches, the porcupine first rattles its spines as a warning. If this fails, the porcupine runs towards the attacker and drives the sharp spines into its flesh.

◀ The skunk's black-and-white-pattern is a warning that it can spray a horrible fluid.

▼ Its legs and belly are unprotected, but if attacked the armadillo rolls into tight ball.

Head and tail fit together to make an armoured 'ball'

Danger past, the armadillo begins to unfurl!

The armadillo walks away

460 The skunk defends itself with a bad-smelling fluid. This fluid comes from special glands near the animal's tail. If threatened, the skunk lifts its tail and sprays its enemy. The fluid's strong smell irritates the victim's eyes and makes it hard to breathe, and the skunk runs away.

I DON'T BELIEVE IT!

Skunks sometimes feed on bees. They roll the bees on the ground to remove their stings before eating them.

461 A rhinoceros may charge at its enemies at top speed.

Rhinos are generally peaceful animals but a female will defend her calf fiercely. If the calf is threatened, she will gallop towards the enemy with her head down and lunge with her sharp horns. Few predators will stay around to challenge an angry rhino.

◄ The sight of a full-grown rhinoceros charging is enough to make most predators turn and run.

462 The pangolin's body is protected by tough overlapping scales.

These make the animal look like a giant pinecone. The pangolin feeds mainly on ants and termites and its thick scales protect it from the stinging bites of its tiny prey.

◄ Even the pangolin's long, prehensile (grasping) tail is well protected.

Deep in the jungle

463 Jungle mammals live at all levels of the forest from the tallest trees to the forest floor. Bats fly over the tree tops and monkeys and apes swing from branch to branch. Lower down, smaller creatures, such as civets and pottos, hide in the dense greenery.

▼ The Amazon rainforest echoes at dawn and dusk with howler monkey whoops and screeches.

464 The howler monkey has the loudest voice in the jungle. Each troop of howler monkeys has its own special area, called a territory. Males in rival troops shout at each other to defend their territory. Their shouts can be heard from nearly 5 kilometres away.

▼ Unlike most cats, jaguars like water, where they hunt for fish, turtles and snakes.

465 The jaguar is one of the fiercest hunters in the jungle. It lives in the South American rainforest and is the largest cat in South America. The pig-like peccary and the capybara – a large jungle rodent – are among its favourite prey.

468 Some monkeys have a long tail that they use as an extra limb when climbing. This is called a prehensile tail. It contains a powerful system of bones and muscles so it can be used for gripping.

◄ Sloths live in Central and South American rainforests and swamps – they are surprisingly good swimmers.

466 The sloth hardly ever comes down to the ground. This jungle creature lives hanging from a branch by its special hook-like claws. It is so well adapted to this life that its fur grows downwards – the opposite way to that of most mammals – so that rainwater drips off more easily.

469 The okapi uses its long tongue to pick leaves from forest trees. This tongue is so long that the okapi can even lick its own eyes clean!

► Okapis feed in dense, remote rainforests in Central Africa.

467 Tapirs are pig-like animals that live on the jungle floor. There are three different kinds of tapir in the South American rainforests and one kind in the rainforests of Southeast Asia. Tapirs have long, bendy snouts and they feed on leaves, buds and grass.

◄ The Brazilian tapir is often found near water and is a good swimmer.

Strange foods

▼ The vampire bat feeds for about 30 minutes, and probably drinks about 26 litres of blood a year.

470 Some mammals only eat one or two kinds of food. The giant panda feeds mainly on the shoots and roots of the bamboo plant. It spends up to 12 hours a day eating, and consumes about 12 kilograms of bamboo a day. The panda also eats small amounts of other plants and sometimes hunts mice and fish.

▶ Giant pandas live in the bamboo forests of central China. There are very few pandas left in the wild, perhaps between 1500 and 3000.

471 The vampire bat feeds on blood — it is the only bat that has this special diet. This bat hunts at night. It finds a victim such as a horse or cow and crawls up its leg onto its body. The bat shaves away a small area of flesh and, using its long tongue, laps up blood that flows from the wound.

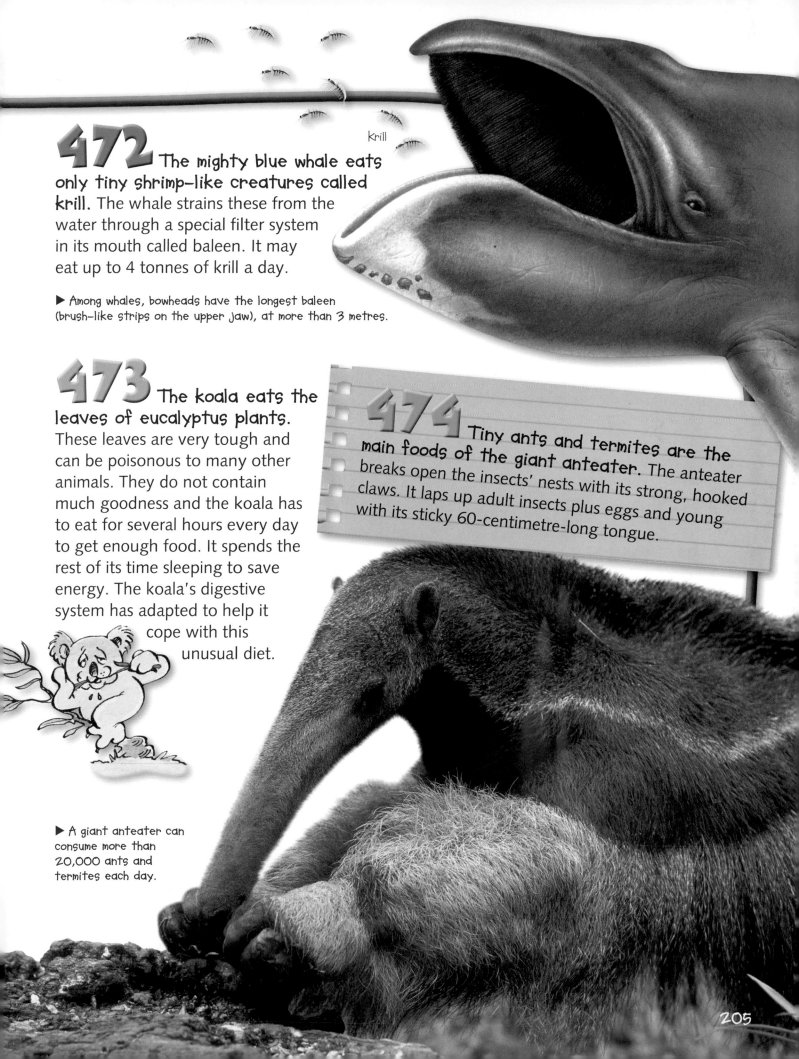

Krill

472 The mighty blue whale eats only tiny shrimp-like creatures called krill. The whale strains these from the water through a special filter system in its mouth called baleen. It may eat up to 4 tonnes of krill a day.

▶ Among whales, bowheads have the longest baleen (brush-like strips on the upper jaw), at more than 3 metres.

473 The koala eats the leaves of eucalyptus plants. These leaves are very tough and can be poisonous to many other animals. They do not contain much goodness and the koala has to eat for several hours every day to get enough food. It spends the rest of its time sleeping to save energy. The koala's digestive system has adapted to help it cope with this unusual diet.

474 Tiny ants and termites are the main foods of the giant anteater. The anteater breaks open the insects' nests with its strong, hooked claws. It laps up adult insects plus eggs and young with its sticky 60-centimetre-long tongue.

▶ A giant anteater can consume more than 20,000 ants and termites each day.

Tool users

475 The chimpanzee is one of the few mammals to use tools to help it find food. It uses a stone like a hammer to crack nuts, and makes use of sticks to pull down fruit from the trees and for fighting. It also uses sticks to help catch insects, for example, by jabbing them into holes in trees to get out grubs, moths and wild bee honey.

◄ The chimp pokes a sharp stick into a termite or ant nest. It waits a moment or two and then pulls the stick out, covered with juicy insects that it can eat.

I DON'T BELIEVE IT!

The cusimanse is a clever kind of mongoose. When it comes across a meal that has a tough shell, it throws it between its hind legs against a stone or tree to break it open and get at the tasty insides!

476 Dolphins show many kinds of intelligent behaviour, including tool use. Some dolphins tear bits of sea sponge from rocks and hold or place them over their snouts, then prod and probe among rocks and sand to find fish and other prey. The sponge prevents the dolphin scratching or hurting its snout.

▶ Dolphins that have learnt to use sponges swap skills with each other, and may even swap sponges.

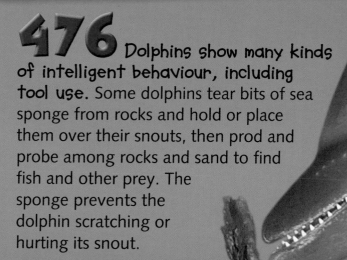

▼ A sea otter smashes a shellfish against a rock to get at the juicy flesh inside.

477 The sea otter uses a stone to break open its shellfish food. It feeds mainly on sea creatures with hard shells, such as mussels, clams and crabs. The sea otter lies on its back in the water and places a rock on its chest. It then bangs the shellfish against the rock until the shell breaks, allowing the otter to get at the soft flesh inside.

City creatures

478 Foxes are among the few larger mammals that manage to survive in towns and cities. They used to find their food in the countryside, but now more and more have discovered that city rubbish bins are a good hunting ground. The red fox will eat almost anything. It kills birds, rabbits, eats insects, fruit and berries and takes human leftovers.

I DON'T BELIEVE IT!
Rats will eat almost anything. They have been known to chew through electrical wires, lead piping and even concrete dams. In the US, rats may cause up to more than one billion dollars' worth of damage every year!

◄ The red fox has spread to all continents except South America and Antarctica, following humans as they throw away food refuse.

▼ The house mouse hides under floors and in cupboards. It will eat any human food it can find, as well as paper, glue and even soap!

479 Rats and mice are among the most successful of all mammals. They live all over the world and eat almost any kind of food. The brown rat and the house mouse are among the most common. The brown rat eats seeds, fruit and grain, but it will also attack birds and mice. In cities it lives in cellars and sewers – anywhere there is rotting food and rubbish.

▼ Young raccoons quickly learn to tip over rubbish bins and tear open plastic bags to get at meal leftovers.

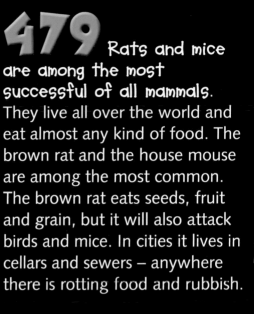

480 Raccoons also live in city areas and raid rubbish bins for food. Like foxes, they eat lots of different kinds of food, including fish, nuts, seeds, berries and insects, as well as what they scavenge from humans. They are usually active at night and spend the day in a den made in a burrow, a hole in rocks or even in the corner of an empty city building.

Freshwater mammals

481 Most river mammals spend only part of their time in water. Creatures such as the river otter and the water rat live on land and go into the water to find food. The hippopotamus, on the other hand, spends most of its day in water to keep cool. Its skin needs to stay moist, and it cracks if it gets too dry.

482 At night hippos leave their river or lake to chomp on land plants. However they rarely stray far and gallop back to water if danger threatens.

483 The water vole makes its home in a bankside burrow. It eats plants growing near the water and in the shallows, and is an expert swimmer.

▲ The water vole has a blunt nose, and furry ears and tail, unlike the brown rat, for which it is often mistaken.

484 The platypus uses its duck-like beak to find food on the riverbed. This strange beak is extremely sensitive to touch and to tiny electric currents given off by prey. The platypus dives down to the bottom of the river and digs in the mud for creatures such as worms and shrimps.

◀ When a platypus has found its food, it stores it in its cheeks until it has time to eat it.

485 The otter's ears close off when it is swimming. This stops water getting into them when the otter dives. Other special features are webbed feet, and short, thick fur, which keeps the otter's skin dry.

486 Most dolphins are sea creatures but some live in rivers. There are four different kinds of river dolphins living in rivers in Asia and South America. The baiji of China is now considered to be extinct. All feed on fish and shellfish. They probably use echolocation, a kind of sonar like that used by bats, to find their prey.

▼ The hippo is not a good swimmer but it can walk on the riverbed. It can stay underwater for up to half an hour.

Plant-eaters

487 In order to get enough nourishment, plant-eaters must spend much of their time eating. A zebra spends at least half its day munching grass. The advantage of being a plant-eater, though, is that the animal does not have to chase and compete for its food like hunters do.

▼ The Mexican long-tongued bat flaps its wings fast to hover in front of flowers as it feeds.

488 Some kinds of bat feed on pollen and nectar. The Queensland blossom bat, for example, has a long brush-like tongue that it plunges deep into flowers to gather its food. As it feeds it pollinates the flowers – it takes the male pollen to the female parts of a flower so that it can bear seeds and fruits.

▼ Carnivores, such as lions, feed on plant-eaters, such as zebras. So there must always be more plant-eaters than carnivores for this 'food chain' to work successfully.

489 Plants are the main foods of most monkeys. Monkeys live in tropical forests where there are plenty of fresh leaves and ripe fruit all year round. Some also eat insects and other small creatures.

◄ Seeds and fruit are the main foods of the red uakari, which lives in South American rainforests.

490 Rabbits have strong teeth for eating leaves and bark. The large front teeth are called incisors and are used for biting leaves and twigs. The incisors keep growing throughout the rabbit's life – if they did not they would wear out. Rabbits also have broad teeth for chewing.

491 The manatee is a water-living mammal that feeds on plants. There are three different kinds of these large, gentle creatures: two live in fresh water in West Africa and in the South American rainforest, and the third lives in the west Atlantic, from Florida to the Amazon.

► Manatees, and their relations dugongs, feed on plants such as water weeds, water lilies and seaweeds.

I DON'T BELIEVE IT!
Manatees are said to have been the origin of sailors' stories about mermaids. Short-sighted sailors may have mistaken these plump sea creatures for beautiful women.

Digging deep

KEY

1 Anti-flood wall around entrance

2 Side chamber

3 Food store

4 Members greet by 'kissing'

5 Nursery chamber

6 Rest/sleep chamber

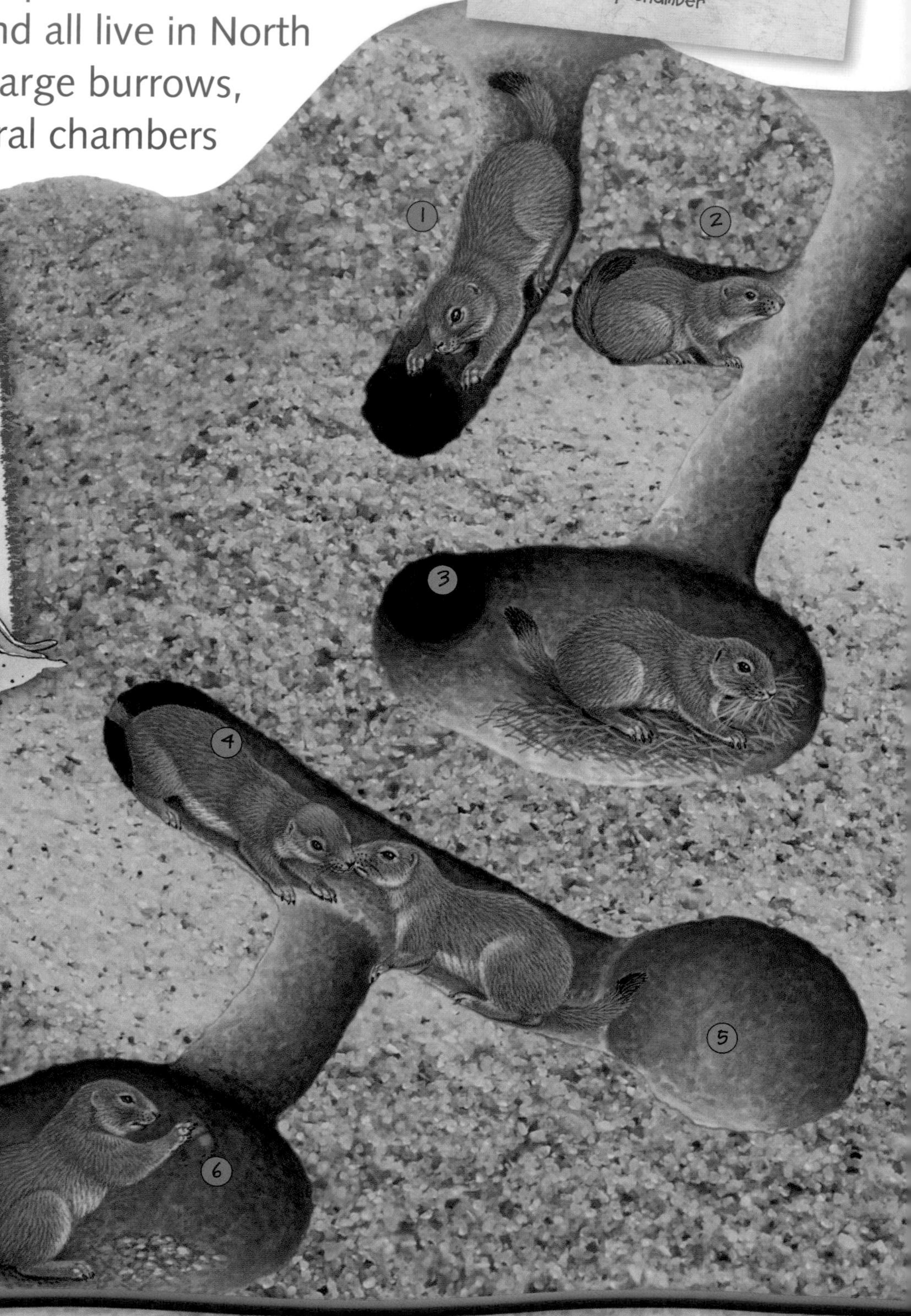

492 Prairie dogs are champion burrowers. These little animals are a kind of plump short-tailed squirrel. There are five different species, and all live in North America. They dig large burrows, which contain several chambers linked by tunnels.

I DON'T BELIEVE IT!

Prairie dogs are not always safe underground. Sometimes burrowing owls move into part of a burrow and then prey on the prairie dogs already living there.

▶ This cutaway view shows the complicated layout of a prairie dog burrow.

493 Badgers dig a network of chambers and tunnels called a sett. There are special areas for breeding, sleeping and food stores. Sleeping areas are lined with dry grass and leaves, which the badgers sometimes take outside to air for a while.

▼ Badgers usually stay in their burrow during the day and come out at dusk. They are playful creatures and adults are often seen playing with their cubs.

▼ The star-nosed mole's sensitive feelers find prey by touch.

494 Moles have specially adapted front feet for digging. The feet are broad and turn outward for pushing through the soil, and the claws are large and strong. Moles have very poor sight. Their sense of touch is well developed and they has sensitive bristles on their faces.

215

Mothers and babies

495 Most whales are born tail first. If the baby emerged head first it could drown during the birth process. As soon as the baby has fully emerged, the mother, with the help of other females, gently pushes it up to the surface to take its first breath. The female whale feeds her baby on milk, just like other mammals.

▼ For the first months of its life, a young whale, such as this grey whale calf, remains almost touching its mother.

496 Whales are the biggest of all mammal babies. A newborn grey whale is 4 metres long, weighs two-thirds of a tonne, and drinks 200 litres of its mother's milk every day – over two bathtubs full!

497 The Virginia opossum may have more than 15 babies at one time – more than any other mammal. The young are only a centimetre long, and all of the babies together weigh only a couple of grams.

498 Bears have some of the smallest babies, compared to the mother's size, of all placental mammals. A newborn giant panda weighs just 120 grams, while its mother can weigh up to 120 kilograms – 1000 times heavier. The length of pregnancy for the mother sloth bear is about seven months. Like other bears, she usually has just one or two offspring in each litter.

◄ A mother sloth bear carries her young on her back until they are perhaps one year old.

500 Baby mammals needs lots of care. The young of many hunting mammals, from tiny weasels to wolves, bears and the biggest cats, are born furless, helpless, and unable to see and hear properly. The mother keeps them safe in a nest or den and returns between hunting to provide milk.

499 Some babies have to be up and running less than an hour after birth. If the young of animals such as antelopes were as helpless as the baby panda they would immediately be snapped up by predators. They must get to their feet and be able to move with the herd as quickly as possible or they will not survive.

► A newborn bison struggles to its feet minutes after birth – wolves or cougars may be near.

217

INDEX

INDEX

ACKNOWLEDGEMENTS

The publishers would like to thank the following sources for the use of their photographs:
t = top, b = bottom, l = left, r = right, c = centre, bg = background, m = main, rt = repeated throughout

Cover: *Front* (t) holbox/Shutterstock.com, (b) Thomas Marent/Minden Pictures/FLPA; *Spine* Abhindia/Shutterstock.com;
Back (c) gfdunt/Shutterstock.com, (l) FloridaStock/Shutterstock.com, (r) Cathy Keifer/Shutterstock.com, (b) Eric Isselee/Shutterstock.com

Alamy 55 Zuma Press, Inc.; 76(b) Brandon Cole Marine Photography; 90–91 Reinhard Dirscherl; 169(t) david tipling

Ardea 89(tc) Valerie Taylor; 104(tr) Ken Lucas

Corbis 112(t) Gary Meszaros/Visuals Unlimited; 124(bl) David A. Northcott; 142–143(m) DLILLC; 142(b) Kevin Schafer; 164(t) John Carnemolla; 171(cr) Rick Price; 205(b) Tom Brakefield; 214 Ocean

Dreamstime.com 37(bc) Paop; 42(c) Cathy Keifer; 57 Naluphoto; 139(t) Chmelars; 155(t) Thesmid; 165(b) Lukyslukys; 172(b) Steve Byland

FLPA 26(t) Bob Gibbons; 29(bc) Christian Ziegler/Minden Pictures; 34(bc) Alfred Schauhuber/Imagebroker; 39(b) Albert Visage; 62–63 Stephen Belcher/Minden Pictures; 90(bl) Biosphoto, Jeffrey Rotman/Biosphoto; 95(table br) Michael & Patricia Fogden/Minden Pictures; 96–97 Fred Bavendam/Minden Pictures; 99(bl) Emanuele Biggi; 101(t) Bruno Cavignaux/Biosphoto; 107(b) Foto Natura Stock; 120 Tui De Roy/Minden Pictures; 122–123 Pete Oxford/Minden Pictures; 127(l) Piotr Naskrecki/Minden Pictures; 130–131 Cyril Ruoso/Minden Pictures; 132–133 Nicolas-Alain Petit/Biosphoto; 133(tl) IMAGEBROKER,INGO SCHULZ/Imagebroker; 138(b) Kevin Elsby; 141(b) Roger Tidman; 144(b) David Hosking; 147(b) ImageBroker/Imagebroker; 158–159(m) Horst Jegen/Imagebroker; 160(b) ImageBroker/Imagebroker; 162(m) Jurgen & Christine Sohns; 163(t) Konrad Wothe/Minden Pictures; 167(b) Shem Compion; 171(t) Dieter Hopf/Imagebroker; 174–175(m) Terry Whittaker; 185(b) Norbert Wu/Minden Pictures; 196(t) Imagebroker, Konrad Wothe; 197(b) ImageBroker/Imagebroker; 203(br) Mark Newman; 207(c) Yann Hubert/Biosphoto; 209(b) Michael Durham/Minden Pictures; 215 John Eveson

Fotolia.com 94(table tr) Becky Stares, (table cl) reb, (table bl) Eric Gevaert, (table br) SLDigi; 96(panel tr rt) Alexey Khromushin; 99(tl) Shane Kennedy; 107(panel cl) Konstantin Sutyagin; 123(panel tr) Irochka; 165(t, bg) pdtnc

Glow Images 8(c) F. Rauschenbach/F1online; 25(c) Rolf Nussbaumer; 27(cl) Meul, J./Arco Images GmbH; 41(tc) Meul, J./Arco Images GmbH; 184(c) SuperStock; 195(b) Terry Whittaker/FLPA; 208 Juniors Bildarchiv; 212(cl) Rolf Nussbaumer

iStockphoto.com 5(tl) & 36(c) Paija; 13(tr) Cathy Keifer; 150–151(bg) ElsvanderGun

National Geographic Creative 67(t) & 82 Jim Abernathy; 87 Paul Sutherland; 89 Brian J. Skerry; 145(cl) Tim Laman; 148(b) Klaus Nigge; 180(l) Hiroya Minakuchi/Minden Pictures; 187(c) Tim Laman; 203(b) Nicole Duplaix

naturepl.com 12(tr) Meul/ARCO; 15(bl) Nature Production; 16(c) Stephen Dalton; 17(tl) Stephen Dalton; 19(c) Visuals Unlimited; 32(r) John Cancalosi; 45(b) Kim Taylor; 50–51, 58 & 79(t) Doug Perrine; 70–71 Bruce Rasner/Rotman; 72(b) David Fleetham; 79(cr) Georgette Douwma; 81(t) Alex Mustard; 102(tr) Jurgen Freund; 103(b) Laurie Campbell; 109(br) Dave Watts; 114(c) Tim MacMillan/John Downer Pro; 115(t) Stephen Dalton; 118–119 Bence Mate; 122(cl) Michael Richards/John Downer; 128(bl) John Cancalosi; 133(br) Visuals Unlimited; 147(t) Mark Carwardine; 166(m) Rolf Nussbaumer; 173(cr) Andrew Walmsley; 176–177 T.J. Rich; 199(t) Andy Rouse, (b) Jabruson; 201(r) Jabruson; 204(tr) Jim Clare

Photoshot 59; 84 Oceans Image; 98(bl) NHPA; 116 NHPA; 125(t) NHPA; 191(c) Imago

Science Photo Library 52–53 Andy Murch/Visuals Unlimited, inc; 54–55 Jaime Chirinos; 73(b) David Fleetham, Visuals Unlimited; 80(t) Andy Murch/Visuals Unlimited, inc.; 207(b) Thomas & Pat Leeson

SeaPics 65(cr) Hirose, (b) Espen Rekdal

Shutterstock.com 1 & 92–93 Eric Isselee; 2–3 Hung Chung Chih; 6(cl) & 93(t) Anneka; 6(cr) & 165(panel tl) Anton_Ivanov; 11(r) Tan Hung Meng; 13(bc) Geanina Bechea; 14(bg) Aleksandr Kurganov, (bl) jps, (c) Marco Uliana; 16(bg) Triff; 17(b) Mark Carrel; 18(c) Smit; 20(tr) Sue Robinson; 21(tr) Dirk Ercken; 22(bg) fotoslaz; 23(br) Steve Byland; 24(tr) jcwait; 26(bg) Jorge Moro, (bl) dabjola, (cl) Rasmus Holmboe Dahl; 27(tr) Nick Stubbs, (bc) Henrik Larsson; 31(tl) Csati; 33(cl) Matt Jeppson, (t) IrinaK, (bl) Narisa Koryanyong; 34(bg) Triff; 35(cr) xpixel, (cl) Glenn Jenkinson; 38(bg) Dr. Morley Read, (c) Eric Isselee; 40(cl) r.classen; 44(bl) Lidara; 46(bl) Cosmin Manci; 47(tc) blewisphotography; 48(c) LilKar; 49(bl) np; 56(b) cbpix; 58(tr) Greg Amptman; 59(t) A Cotton Photo; 60–61 Rich Carey; 61(b) NatalieJean; 63(cl) BW Folsom, (br) cdelacy; 65(tr) Sedin; 66(b) Greg Amptman; 67(b) cbpix; 68–69 Brandelet; 71 L.Watcharapol; 72(t) Krzysztof Odziomek; 74 Rich Carey; 76(tr) FAUP, (map) L.Watcharapol; 79(b) BMCL; 80(b) Christophe Rouziou; 81(b) cbpix; 82–83 Rich Carey; 82 & 83 FAUP; 85 iliuta goean; 86–87 tororo reaction; 88(b) Arend van der Walt, (tr) Alex Pix; 91 Ru Bai Le; 94 Joe Farah; 95 Mircea Bezergheanu, (table t) Dirk Ercken, (table cl) Brandon Alms, (table cr) Salim October, (table bl) Jason Mintzer; 97(tr) iliuta goean; 98–99 Brian Lasenby; 98(paper br rt) monbibi; 101(bl) AdStock RF; 103(panel tr) Asaf Eliason; 104–105 Meister Photos; 105(chameleon) Brandon Alms, (tree frog) Eduard Kyslynskyy; 107(tr) infografick; 108(b) Manja; 109(tl) clearviewstock; 110–111 Ivan Kuzmin; 110(b) Statsenko; 111(bl) Anneka; 112(b) Cathy Keifer; 113 worldswildlifewonders; 114–115(bg) Iakov Kalinin; 114(b) Madlen; 116(bl) J. L. Levy; 121(bg) Rich Carey; 126 alslutsky; 127(cr) Eric Isselee; 129(bl) Audrey Snider-Bell; 134–135(m) Atul Sinai Borker; 136(t) Grant Glendinning, (l–r) Florian Andronache, Eduardo Rivero, Clinton Moffat, (b, bg) nuttakit; 137(b) BMJ; 138(m) Sergei25, (b, bg) monbibi; 140(b) ktsdesign; 141(t) AndreAnita; 143(t) WayneDuguay; 144–145(t) Eric Isselee; 146–147 Alfredo Maiquez; 150(t) Gregg Williams, (b) Arto Hakola, (tr, bl) Johan Swanepoel, (tl, br) monbibi; 151(cl) Johan Swanepoel, (b) monbibi; 153(t) tntphototravis, (b) Stu Porter, (bg) T.Allendorf; 154(m) Jerome Whittingham; 155(b) Kimberley McClard; 157(t) picturepartners, (b) IbajaUsap; 159(b) David Dohnal; 160(t) Gentoo Multimedia Limited; 161(t) Jan de Wild, (b) Karel Gallas; 162(t, bg) monbibi; 163(bl) & (br) worldswildlifewonders; 164–165 John Carnemolla; 165(panel tr) Eric Isselee, (panel br) Jason Mintzer; 166(b) Richard Fitzer; 167(tl) zimmytws; 168 FloridaStock; 170–171 Rob McKay; 173(tl) fotofactory; 174(t) You Touch Pix of EuToch, (t, b); 175(t) monbibi; 178 Norma Cornes; 179(t) BMJ, (tc) Smileus, (b) Incredible Arctic; 181(b) CHAINFOTO24; 182(bl) Neil Burton, (c) Mark Beckwith; 184–185(c) jaytee; 186–187(c) Sarun T; 188(c) Incredible Arctic, (b) Magdanatka; 189(b) Zoltan Katona; 193(t) Erni; 194(t) outdoorsman; 194(b) EcoPrint; 196–197 Bozena Fulawka; 198(b) Mogens Trolle; 200(b) Ultrashock; 202(tr) BMJ; 202–203 theerapol sri-in; 203(tl) Eric Isselee; 209(t) TranceDrumer; 210–211(b) Anna Omelchenko; 211(t) worldswildlifewonders; 212(b) EcoPrint; 213(b) Andrea Izzotti; 217(b) Jean-Edouard Rozey

Superstock 145(br) Biosphoto

All other photographs are from: digitalSTOCK, digitalvision, ImageState, John Foxx, PhotoAlto, PhotoDisc, PhotoEssentials, PhotoPro, Stockbyte

All artworks from the Miles Kelly Artwork Bank

Every effort has been made to acknowledge the source and copyright holder of each picture. Miles Kelly Publishing apologizes for any unintentional errors or omissions.